THE STRUGGLE FOR BASIC NEEDS IN NEPAL

THE STRUGGLE FOR BASIC NEEDS IN NEPAL

by

P.M. Blaikie

J.Cameron

J. Seddon

Adroit Publishers

Delhi - 110 053

Published by
ADROIT PUBLISHERS
C-8/2, Yamuna Vihar, Delhi-110 053
e-mail: akhilbooks@yahoo.com
Phone: 3266030

ISBN : 81-87392-16-9

Layout by
Sudhir Kumar Vatsa

Laser Typeset by
Nidhi Laser Point, Shahdara, Delhi.
e-mail: nidhi_vatsa@hotmail.com
Phone : 2825424

Printed in India by
B.K. Offset, Shahdara Delhi-110 032

PREFACE[1]

Well before official international attention was focused on the basic needs approach, the Development Centre of the OECD was interested in the strategies which affect the poorest groups in the Third World. As early as 1874, a seminar on this topic was convened at the Centre.[2] In 1975 a wide-ranging collective study was initiated to examine both the theoretical foundations and the concrete features of alternative development schemes for the provision of basic goods and services.[3]

The project of which the present study is part, *Basic Needs: General Aspects and National Contexts*, was started in 1976, shortly after the World Employment Conference's call to include as priority objective of development the promotion of employment and the satisfaction of basic needs of each country's population.

Most of the research resources devoted by international organisations to the new strategy were concentrated on economic and technical studies. A whole area remained for the Centre to explore: the social and political dimensions of basic-needs policies.

In a first meeting of international experts it was decided to launch a series of case studies on the relationship between national and international political and social aspects of underdevelopment and the satisfaction of basic needs at the level of the village, the neighbourhood and the household.

To respect to the utmost the autonomy of the local teams and to benefit from the considerable experience of each in a particular national context, the Centre avoided the easy course of determining a priori the research topics and imposing pre-conceived guidelines. Instead, it arranged a succession of meetings in which the researchers could discuss both substantial issues and problems of research design with a rotating group of international experts, so that a consensus could arise on common research hypotheses and on the broad lines of a shared methodology. This provided a sound basis for comparison, in spite of the specificity of the different case studies.

Eight study proposals were formulated; four of them materialised in the monographs which will be published in the present series.

All of them focus on the socio-economic, political and cultural relationships of specific deprived groups with the rest of the society, in the context of their national and local social history. The groups are defined in terms of their position in the process of production - and not on the basis of cutting points in a statistical distribution - and an effort is made to portray concretely their power relationships, as they fight the aggressions of their social and political environment and try to survive and to shape a place for themselves.

Each study tries to capture the interrelationships between deprivation at the village and household level, on the one hand, and national and international long-range processes, on the other, by using not only economic statistics and social and political history but interviews, life histories, informal local history and other anthropological data.

Besides the present one, the project has resulted in three other case studies:

Basic Needs in India: A View From Above and From Below of Karnataka State's Policies[4] explores two aspects of basic-needs strategies in the context of the South India State of Karnataka. Part I discusses the scene at the "macro" level and examines how a number of political decisions have been translated into action. Part II investigates how the poor themselves struggle to survive. Both parts complement each other and cast light on the way development is perceived at one pole of society and implemented at the other.

Basic Needs in the Context of Social Changes: The Case of Peru[5] underlines the changing structural determinants of the life conditions of two groups of agricultural workers selected to illustrate the differentiation of the poor in Peru and their changing individual and collective strategies for basic-needs satisfaction. The study shows that the life conditions of the selected groups are largely dependent on their relationships with outside groups and institutions and that these relationships change as a result of the convergence between structural transformation and local efforts.

"Tarahil" and Landless Labourers in Rural Egypt[6] studies the end result of policies adopted by the Egyptian Government after the 1958 military revolution, on behalf of the lowest income groups of that country, including land reform, subsidies, price fixing, etc. The groups chosen to pinpoint the effects of those policies are the "tarahil", migrant labour gangs formed by landless and almost land-less peasants, recruited seasonally by labour contractors, and working as a group away from their villages of origin.

Besides the four case-study reports, the present series will include an analytical bibliography of the basic-needs literature, with a critical commentary[7], and a final synthesis by the co-ordinator and editor of the project, Denyse Harari.

Professor Louis SABOURIN

NOTES

1. The present study has been jointly sponsored and financed by the Development Centre of the OECD and the Directorate for Development Co-operation and Humanitarian Assistance of the Foreign Affairs Department of the Swiss Confederation.

   We want to express here our thanks also to the ILO, the IBRD, the IDS and to many of their individual members for the generous intellectual and logistical support the project received from them.

2. Seminar on Development Projects designed to Reach the Lowest Income Groups: OECD Development Centre, Paris, 17th-19th June, 1974.

3. Robert Cassen and Margaret Wolfson (Eds), 1978, *Planning for Growing Populations*. Paris: OECD Development Centre.

4. T.S. Epstein, M.N. Panini, M.N. Srinivas, V.S. Parthasarathy, 1980, OECD Development Centre (forthcoming).

5. Giogio Alberti, 1980, OECD Development Centre (forthcoming).

6. Provisional Title. By Sawsan El-Messiri (forthcoming).

7. Jorge Garcia-Bouza, May 1980, *A Basic Needs Analytical Bibliography*, OECD Development Centre.

SUMMARY

This study on the struggle for basic needs in Nepal is based on two periods of field work. The first period involved five man-years of research during 1974-75, the purpose of which was to evaluate the socio-economic impact of road construction; a wide range of surveys, subject-specific investigations, and detailed case-studies were undertaken. One of the surveys, a household and production survey of 667 rural households provided the major data base from which a sub-sample was selected later for the basic needs study.

During the second period of field work which took place in 1978 the same households were revisited and open-ended interviews were carried out to discover the form and extent of their struggles for basic needs; their survival strategies, forms of communal action, and attempts to achieve control over production in the widest sense; their economic, social and political relations with others; as well as quantitative data on earnings, consumption, assets, etc. (to be compared with our 1974-75 information).

A review of current official documents relating to public policy, foreign aid strategies, and an up-dating from secondary sources of the authors' understanding of the political economy of Nepal was also undertaken during the second visit.

The groups concerned by the study are the most deprived and poor people in one of the poorest countries of the world. Although they constitute an extreme case, their situation has many of the economic and social features characteristic of underdevelopment. They are held in social and economic relations which maintain their poverty, which is rapidly deepening because of the crisis associated with stagnant production and increasing population. Their attempts to withdraw from these relations, or to manipulate them to their best advantage have by and large, not yet amounted to a politically conscious and organised attempt to transform the fundamental structures which at present imprison them in dependence and deprivation.

Rather, their actions amount to survival strategies, usually carried out on an individual basis. These individual actions usually involve the increased use of resources of land and forest, which, under currently prevailing technical conditions and property relations, cannot support even the present population.

The report seeks to identify both the contradictions in the political economy of Nepal which constrain the transformation of society along the lines of suggestions which already appear in official and academic documents and current political debates (popular participation, representation of the majority of the population, increasing communal control over resources and production decisions), which would be necessary if a basic needs strategy is to be adopted, and the positive influences which might help bring into being such a strategy.

FOREWORD

Introduction

We are very pleased to see The Struggle for Basic Needs in Nepal reprinted twenty years after its original publication in 1979 by the OECD Development Centre in Paris, and made available (as the earlier edition was not) to readers in Nepal and the rest of South Asia. The study on which the book is based was undertaken in 1978 following nearly two years of fieldwork in what was then West Central Nepal during 1974 and 1975. But it remains, we believe, surprisingly relevant today, twenty years later, despite the many changes in the rural areas of Nepal and in approaches to rural change.

The *Struggle for Basic Needs in Nepal* is about the struggles of poor rural people to survive under 'conditions not of their own choosing' but in those established by a complex set of factors - economic, social and political - which together constitute the political economy of Nepal. The book constructs this political economy, with a brief historical introduction leading to its contemporary structure and dynamics in the 1970s. But the major focus of the work is on the lives, and what today might be called the livelihoods, of a sub-sample of the poorest and most socially disadvantaged rural and urban individuals and households from a larger sample taken in the course of a major project in the West Central Region of Nepal (which gave rise to several books, including *Peasants and Workers in Nepal, and Nepal in Crisis).*

The emphasis is not on the individuals and households seen as 'economic agents' in a market constrained only by imperfections in the market, as the current neo-liberal orthodoxy would claim. It is about real people struggling - as the poor and socially disadvantaged are obliged to struggle - by force of circumstance, to survive and to hold onto what few resources they have, to enlarge where possible their room for manoeuvre within existing conditions and even to attempt (albeit with great difficulty and usually unsuccessfully) to improve the material conditions of their lives.

Much of the discussion focuses the structural conditions under which decision-making and strategies for survival are made, and on the ways in which the poor struggle to ensure the fulfilment of their basic needs. Few of the poor and socially disadvantaged are able to move beyond this minimum goal, although most aspire to gain a greater degree of security or range of options. Still less did they succeed in changing the conditions under which they live in a more systematic and sustained fashion.

In 1996/7, the authors re-surveyed the parts of Nepal where the basic needs research was undertaken in 1978and the results of which will be published in full. Overall, it is perhaps the lack of dramatic change in the conditions of existence for many households in West Nepal over the years from 1974/75 to 1996/97 that is the most striking - and depressing - feature of the results from this survey.

It is in the nature of untargeted surveys that they give the clearest image of the middle of the distribution, if there is a significant concentration in the central ground. Results tend to be quoted in terms of averages and significant proportions of cases. Both the rare accumulating rich household and the desperately poor household are likely to be missed and/or treated as difficult exceptions. This bias was avoided in

Struggle, since the most vulnerable were specifically selected for follow-up in the fieldwork for this book.. However, the numerous forms of error involved in all surveys are, of course, shared, and must make any conclusions very tentative.

Nevertheless, after twenty years or so, it is difficult to dismiss the impression that Nepalese rural society, at least in West Nepal (now Central Nepal), has a large core of households who have coped quite well. Maintaining a production base in land ownership, they have prudently bought and sold small parcels of land, experimented with fertiliser and improved seed, increased irrigation wherever possible, borrowed or lent moderate amounts of money for investment and consumption, put more children (including some daughters) into formal education, and, maintained simple consumption patterns based on self-provisioning food-security.

The trajectory of this type of cautious, risk-averse experimentation has involved agricultural activities in the *terai,* sometimes after migration from the hills, and with non-agricultural activities in the hills. In both hills and *terai,* the 1996/7 surveys suggest livelihoods trajectories for the "middle peasantry" have been sustainable in the multiple meanings of that word. It seems reasonable to conclude that the economic, political and cultural circumstances faced by the poorest groups in rural society in struggling to meet their basic needs through relationships with their richer neighbours have therefore probably changed little in the past twenty years, with regard to employment, gifts, loans and other patron-client relations, linking the very poor (the focus of *Struggle*), and these more advantaged sections of the middle peasantry.

Have conditions of absolute deprivation improved for the poorest in Nepal?

The people interviewed in 1978 were primarily those who we had found to be virtually or totally landless in a stratified random survey of 665 rural households in then West Central Nepal in 1973/4. The forty-one households interviewed for the basic needs research from these survey households were thus around seven percent of our total in the 1973/4 sample. All our households would certainly have been well below any conceivable poverty line at that time.

Research between 1978 and 1999 can be used to examine whether the poorest ten percent of people in Nepal still live in similar material conditions of absolute poverty. Many groups in Nepal continue to suffer from chronic food insecurity, partly due to a deepening agricultural production malaise:

> "Nepal has gone from being a food exporter to a net importer, and cash crops remain of minor importance ...Yields of almost all key crops have been declining, with the limited increases in output accounted for mainly by expansion of cropped area into more marginal lands." (World Bank 1991: 27)

The extent of the problem in Nepal is indicated by NPC estimates that 43 percent of the population consumed below the poverty line level of 2250 calories per day per capita in 1984/85. By 1992/93, this proportion of a larger population was estimated to have risen to 49 percent (An Outline of Poverty Alleviation Policies and Programmes; NPC, May 1993: Kathmandu; page 1).

Chronic food insecurity is suggested too, by anthropometric surveys in the Kosi Hills in the early 1980s by the KHARDEP project and SCF-UK:—

> "The weights of adult men and women fell between harvest and monsoon in all sites. The fall was greater for adults from poorer families. Average weights of children also tended to be lower in the monsoon visit; most children were thinner at this time. Children from poorer families were more likely to suffer from delayed growth (stunting) than children from wealthier families; 20% of children from poorer families were severely stunted in November 1981 (as compared to 13% of children from wealthier families). Children from wealthier families were more likely to be wasted."
> (The Impact of the Kosi Hill Area Rural Development

Programme: Description of the data collected in the second year of the KHARDEP Impact Studies - 2038-39 (1981-82); David Nabarro and Mahesh Pant; Coordinator's Office KHARDEP, Dhankuta; 1983; xvi)

Lastly, the National Living Standard Measurement Survey found over forty percent of the population below the poverty line. The poorest ten percent must therefore still be living in conditions of absolute deprivation by any global standards. While for some, the opportunities for employment and income generation outside agriculture and even abroad have increased, and while there have also been continuing changes in potential access as a result of improved transport, to health and education facilities, the struggle for 'basic needs' among the most socially disadvantaged ten percent of households is as real and as desperate as ever.

Have recent political changes changed the lives of the poorest?

The *Struggle for Basic Needs* was very concerned with the distribution of political power and how the poorest were not only excluded as decision-makers, but actively repressed. When we were writing in the 1970s, the fundamental political rights that have now existed formally in Nepal for a decade, were not available. This was the era of the 'Panchayati Raj'. But, although in important ways, the 'coming of democracy' at the national level has crucially altered the parameters of Nepal's political economy, at the 'grassroots' the lives of the rural poor and disadvantaged are not so different today from twenty years ago. While the very disadvantaged are now on the agenda of many policies and projects in the region, the pervasive structural determinants of their poverty, food insecurity and hardship have not been substantially shifted, for all the political reform and explicit concern focused upon them.

Since the installation of multi-party democracy, local development initiatives have become highly politicised, where political parties now vie with each other in all but the minutest allocative decisions at the ward and village level. While there is now a more open and vocal political life in all areas of Nepal, both rural and urban, it represents only increased competition for a share of external funding and to access to existing natural resources such as land, water and forest products, which have not increased through time, and have now to be shared by a population almost two thirds as large again as it was in 1979. However, for the bottom ten percent of the population, it has not been a record of any substantial gain. While there is the intention of many projects, at least on paper and in implementation, to reach this bottom decile, outcomes are disappointing. Two illustrative projects are discussed, and in each case it is the most disadvantaged who have remained excluded from the intended benefits.

In terms of equity, evaluations of Forest User Groups (FUGs) as institutions seen at the cutting edge of the reformed politics of local democracy and redistribution, but indicate that the most food insecure households are experiencing some stress under FUG management. These can take the form of restrictions on physical access or payments to the FUG (e.g. for fuelwood) previously obtained free of monetary cost. The poorest are also marginal to decision-making on both Forest and Water User Groups, even when a member of the household (almost invariably the eldest man) is said to be a member of the Group. The equity aspect demands explicit policy attention in terms of facilitating greater "voice" for women and poorer households, both of which either provide the (hard) for collecting forest products (particularly firewood and fodder) and/or rely on the non-private, common property resources for a larger part of their needs than landed and generally richer households. Government organisations and the bilateral agencies assisting them have showed a varying capacity for this task despite notable successes in facilitating the creation of Forest User Groups in the different parts of Nepal.. Also, for all the share of the aid literature circulating in Kathmandu which Forest Policy occupies, the actual numbers of covered by this programme in Nepal as a whole, is tiny.

In the most general terms, the most food insecure

households in Nepalese society will continue to seek survival and advancement through relationships with other households in the locality - though usually in a highly subordinated role. Their low capacity for self-provisioning means they have household and group interest in the collective life of the locality. Arguably, the more local cooperation, the more the poorest can find opportunities to gain access to new resources.. FUG groups offer, on paper and in intention, a new institutional opportunity for the poor, disadvantaged and for women. Although detailed studies of the distributional impacts of FUGs are still awaited, there are a number of informal reports and statements in the public sphere which suggest that the underlying subordinate position of these groups remains little changed. The policy lesson here is to return to the political economic reality which bears down upon them. The poorest households will tend to operate on two tracks - both relatively independent income generation activities and activities dependent on the agreement of more advantaged actors in the locality. It is important that the first track is not neglected for the second in the name of sustainable environmental management, and the independent income generation priorities of groups of the food insecure are not undermined by restrictive regulation without compensation.

The second example is the the Small Farmers' Development Programme (SFDP), which began in 1975, when the existing Sajha (Cooperatives)s were found to favour larger farmers, and an early critique of the SFDP appears in Struggle. More recent research indicates that SFDP groups have 10 to 25 members, and minimum collateral with a business plan.. By 1991, 115,000 families were being assisted through a network of 450 groups in the first fifteen years of operation. The SFDP programme was evaluated in 1991 (Impact Evaluation of the Small Farmers' Development Programme of Nepal, 1991. Agricultural Credit Division, Development Finance Department, Nepal Rastra Bank; Kathmandu). The results of the evaluation suggested:

(a) Group dynamics remained one of the weakest areas of the SFDP operation. (ibid, v)

(b) "at least 15 per cent [of groups] never held the group meetings after the first loan." (ibid, 191)

(c) "Emphasis on collateral-based financing eroded the concept of collective responsibility..[left individuals exposed] .... The collateral system could also prevent landless farmers and women groups from taking full benefits under the Programme." (ibid, 191)

(d) The problem of deciding whether higher incomes are realy due to SFDP activities (bearing in mind that only 3% were landless and only 50% below owning less than 0.51 ha agricultural land in the hills). However, the project group were found to be better off after the SFDP than the control group.

(e) The problem of continuity and effectiveness of official contact with groups.

(f) Only 1 in 6 groups are women's groups, but two thirds of women who did participate, did take up new activities.

These two examples amongst many others thrived, at least at the inception phase in the favourable climate of the post-democracy reforms policy statement on poverty:

> "Emphasis will be put on increased participation of the beneficiaries in the project development phase and a more demand driven determination of the needs will be introduced in governmental procedures." (An Outline of Poverty Alleviation Policies and Programmes; NPC, May 1993: Kathmandu; 3)

Though the NPC also notes:

> "Any program attempting to reach the poorest of the poor will have to build and develop ad-hoc mechanisms which will take time to become fully operational." (An Outline of Poverty Alleviation Policies and Programmes; NPC, May 1993: Kathmandu; 3)

This positive refocusing of attention is reflected in the following statement from a major international agency:

> "to achieve the overall goals of poverty alleviation, the sustained development of the production potential and the conservation of the natural resource base within a participatory and decentralised control system ..The main implementation principles..which are needed to overcome some of the conditions of administrative malaise inherited from the previous political system: participation, decentralisation, multi-disciplinary team approach, quality of delivery, incentives, sustainability" (FAO 1991: 97)

On the less benign side of the rural experience of the disadvantaged, the National Planning Commission points to an "oppressive socio-cultural tradition" as an aspect of poverty, notably for women (An Outline of Poverty Alleviation Policies and Programmes; NPC, May 1993: Kathmandu; 1). The NPC also recognises the dependence of the poorest on wage labour envisaging Village Labour Banks to enhance "collective bargaining power." (An Outline of Poverty Alleviation Policies and Programmes; NPC, May 1993: Kathmandu; 10).

This finds international support, but with an important structural reason for poverty, namely, land tenure :

> "the poor could fare better ... by freeing up the political and social environment at the village level to allow more self-reliant activity; and by eliminating some of the more exploitative aspects of labour and construction contracting arrangements. Also the current tenancy system provides disincentives both to maximising output, to equitably sharing the costs of inputs, and to allowing security of tenure" (World Bank 1991: 117)

Thus, there appears to be a widespread view that the most are in need of being separately targeted for some policy purposes. A contrary line of argument is pursued by the Agricultural Perspective plan (APP), for example, which takes the view that special facilities are not needed for the poorest households and women. There is little effort here to take into account the difficulties experienced by formal institutions working with groups of the relatively poor, and the enduring conclusion that the poorest households are subject to oppression and exploitative relationships, which circumvent most interventions targeted on them.

The changes since 1991 may have reduced the exercise of outright repression against the poorest by coalitions of civil society interests and state agencies, but there has been little change towards positive access to new resources for the poorest through civil society or the state.

Is basic needs still relevant?

Our research in the 1970s was very critical of what we called the bureaucratic and top-down model of basic needs, in which external agencies defined target populations, measured the gaps for specific goods and services and then designed a delivery mechanism to fill the gaps for the target group. We felt basic needs should be radical in terms of people defining their own basic needs, and politically and practically self-mobilising to demand and meet those needs be met as a matter of natural justice.

Both radical and bureaucratic approaches to basic needs were overtaken by the emergence of neo-liberalism as a development strategy on a global scale in the 1980s. But while the global basic needs debate has been displaced by debates about liberalisation and the benefits to be derived from open market forces, a multi-disciplinary, radical approach to poverty was kept alive in the work of recent Nobel Prize winner, Amartya Sen.

Amartya Sen was not a major contributor to the debates on basic needs as a development strategy that dominated development thinking in the middle and late 1970s. Certainly the publication of Poverty and Famines (Sen, 1981) was a late, if lasting, contribution to understanding the nature of extreme deprivation of basic needs. But it was not in the mainstream of the baisc needs debates of the late 1970s. The debate over basic needs was generally dominated by more subtle interpretations of needs than chronic lack of food and was couched in terms of positive development, rather than ameliorating disaster.

From the early 1980s, Amartya Sen was identified with the United Nations University World Institute for Development Economics Research (WIDER). WIDER became an important institution for innovation in thinking on development economics, but also included social philosophers. The work on famine ran in parallel throughout the 1980s, but the challenge of the WIDER work was to go beyond the self-evident moral horror of famine to more universal statements on inequality . But there is a considerable analytical leap involved in moving from moral horror at unnecessary death to moral indignation at unnecessary inequality.

Neo-classical economists supporting liberalisation claim to be on the side of the free individual with a unique, innate, unmeasurable capacity for feeling desire and innate talents to generate resources to satisfy those desires - a proposition attractive to many people socialised in the west. Sen criticises this assumption as failing to recognise that desire is itself socially constructed and, more ethically, that valuation is separable from desire (Sen, 1985b, 32). His special concern is with those people whose demanding life experience has closed down their desires compared to those whose lives have been more privileged from an early age (Sen, 1985b, 29).

Sen then examines a sequence of conceptual mappings, each of which he would claim could be empirically verified, at least in part (Sen, 1985b, 35);

- from sets of commodities available to an individual to the set of individual's absolute capabilities, involving a dimension of advantage or disadvantage in those capabilities in comparison with others (Sen, 1985, 5);
- from the set of individual capabilities to the set of individual functionings;
- from the set of individual functionings to individual well-being.

At each stage, it can be established that there exists potential for variations in degrees of choice within constraints.

The notion of the degree of choice itself is treated as significant, but not as significant as being able to achieve a set of capabilities that permits functioning consistent with a good life (Sen, 1985b, 14/15 and 67/70). Constraints on capabilities can be seen as entitlement limitations (Sen, 1985b, 27), linking to the work on famine. If adequate nutritional commodities are not received for example, then capabilities (to search for and perform useful work, for example) are constrained. If capabilities are constrained then the capacity to turn commodities into functionings such as good health, is also constrained. If functionings are constrained then the overall level of achievable well-being has a ceiling. Thus, the ill-nourished child becomes the less capable adult disabled from converting what few opportunities are offered into fully functioning outcomes with a resulting low level of lifelong well-being.

Amartya Sen also addressed more socially determined examples of ethically unjust treatment, notably the experience of women. The second Appendix of Commodities and Capabilities is wholly devoted to Amartya Sen's collaborative research into gender discrimination in India as a case study of clear capability damage (Sen and Sengupta, 1983). But even here, the evidence given is of physiological damage in terms of differentials in life expectancy and timely access to health care as a commodity, not the experience of lack of choice (Sen, 1997, 212). Though in this book as in much of his writing, relative deprivation and Adam Smith's concern with the right to the set of commodities consistent with the capability to function "in public without shame", receives acknowledgement as an important criterion for assessing well-being. Amartya Sen's ethical position is that people have rights to the commodities that enhance their capabilities and the right to express those capabilities as fuller functionings to achieve higher wellbeing.

His support of an open mass media, for the prevention of destruction of human capabilities through famine (Sen, 1985, 77), can be extended to support informed political and ethical debate on poverty that has relevance to Nepal in the new political climate. The term "access" appears in other of our publications and is an early precursor of Sen's work. It also has been re-invented in some of the most recent conceptualisations of the "livelihood approach" to rural development. The idea of access however is not explicit but

The parallels between the language of The Struggle for Basic Needs in Nepal (1979) and Amartya Sen's (1998 Nobel Prize Winner for Economics)

Struggle for Basic Needs in Nepal (with page numbers from the original version)	Amartya Sen and the causes of poverty
"As ecological decline and division of land through inheritance continues, it is inevitable that increasing numbers of households are forced on to the labour market in conditions which leave them vulnerable to malnutrition as well as to temporary disabilities and illness, leading to debt and subsequent sale of their few remaining assets" (p.38)	Falling entitlements (loss of rights to resources in times of growing vulnerability/insecurity derived from the acceptance of obligations by others)
"the poor ... are in fact the direct producers whose labour generates the wealth of the country, but who have little control over the means of production or of distribution" (p.42)	Frustrated capabilities (limitations on potential to undertake a range of production and consumption activities that constitute a good life in a given society at a given point in time)
"a basic needs strategy must aim to provide the deprived and poor with a means of escape... not through their identification as a 'target' for assistance from above, but through their own involvement in the process of development" (p.42)	Constrained functionings (limits to actual choice among capabilities, including the degrees to which the there is freedom of choice combining individual liberty with acceptance of entitlements of others as obligations)

implicit in *The Struggle for Basic Needs.* Instead, the focus is on the structural characteristics of the Nepalese political economy, particularly the social relations of production, which constrain the possibilities for improving their lives. These constraints can equally easily be mapped onto the patterning of sets of commodities, capabilities and functionings, and, indeed, provide a political economic explanation of these mappings. Thus we claim this book's conceptual approach of social relations of production, and access to income and survival choices within a sluggish development of the productive forces, is not an outdated one.

Further, the conclusions to *Struggle* pps. (90-97) were prescient of future directions of rural development, towards participation of the very poorest in local development, local determination of needs, assured political representation, and training of local cadres, which have all become mainstream debates in Nepal and elsewhere. Unfortunately too, the material conditions of the very disadvantaged, and the conditions which maintain them is also not dated, since their condition has remained largely unchanged over the past twenty years. For these reasons, *Struggle* has worn reasonably well, and its message are not out of touch either with contemporary development agenda, nor with the material conditions of life in Nepal.

We dedicate our work to all those who work for change and for the progressive transformation of the conditions and circumstances in which the rural poor still struggle for their 'basic needs'.

Piers Blaikie
John Cameron
David Seddon

June 2000

CONTENTS

1
THE CRISIS IN NEPAL

An Introduction to Nepal

The population of Nepal is overwhelmingly rural. In 1971 only some 462,000 out of a total of about 11½ million were living in urban centres of more than 5,000 inhabitants. Nepal's economy is predominantly agrarian, with some 93 per cent of the active population employed in farming and only about 2 per cent involved in non-agricultural production, or industry.[8]

About 5 per cent of the population lives in the Kathmandu Valley, where urban areas of Kathmandu, Patan and Bhadgaon combine to provide the only urban complex of any size in the country (with about 500,000 inhabitants), and where the intensity of cultivation is greater than anywhere else in Nepal.

Outside the Kathmandu Valley, the rural areas may be divided into three major topographic and ecological zones: *the mountains* in the north; *the hills*, lying as a thick double band containing a number of valleys (such as Kathmandu Valley) across the centre of the country; and the narrow strip of low-lying plains *(terai)* in the south. In all, Nepal covers about 140,000 sq.kms, (seeTable 1) although figures for both area and population must be regarded with extreme caution and considered as approximations.

The mountains, although constituting about a quarter of the total land area, are sparsely populated (25 persons per sq.km.) with about 5-7 per cent of Nepal's population. Even so, with the area actually cultivated amounting to probably no more than 3 per cent of all cultivated land in the country, a significant proportion of the mountain population are unable to live from farming alone, and must supplement their income from other sources, including long-distance trade, or else migrate south to the hills and the plains for at least part of the year.

Table 1

POPULATION BY GEOGRAPHIC REGIONS IN 1961 CENSUS

Region	*Area Sq. Km.*	*% of Total Area*	*Population 1961*	*% of Total Populataion*	*Density per Sq. Km.*
Western Mountains and Hills	50,803	36.0	1,796,690	19.2	35
Central Mountains and Hills	28,862	20.5	1,946,502	20.6	67
Eastern Mountains and Hills	30,931	21.9	2,080,388	22.0	67
Western Terai	7,363	5.2	271,551	2.8	37
Central Terai	9,021	6.5	644,593	6.7	71
Eastern Terai	13,247	9.4	2,213,282	23.5	167
Kathmandu Valley	565	0.4	459,990	4.9	815
Nepal	140,792	100.0	9,412,996	100.0	67
Mountains and Hills	110,596	78.4	5,823,580	61.8	53
Terai	29,632	21.1	3,129,426	33.0	106

The hills contain some 60 per cent of Nepal's population but only about a quarter of the cultivated land, ensuring that population density is high in general and extremely high per cultivated hectare.[9] Land holdings tend to be small and fragmented (see Table 2) with cultivation carried out largely on narrow terraces built up the hill sides; yields are low and appear to be declining as soil fertility decreases. The majority of hill districts are "food deficit", obliged to import a considerable proportion of their food grain requirements from the plains or from India, and paying for this with cash earned largely outside the hills, usually abroad.

The plains, or *terai*, account for between 15 per cent and 20 per cent of Nepal's total land area, but as much as 70 per cent of cultivated land, and over 30 per cent of the country's population. Regarded as a prime source of government revenue from as early as the 18th century, the *terai* continues to be the "grain basket" of Nepal, producing a very considerable grain surplus, much of which, however, is exported, legally and illegally, across the border to India.

Table 2

AVERAGE SIZE OF LAND HOLDING BY REGIONS IN NEPAL (1962)

Region	*Average Size of Holding in Hectares*
Nepal	1.23
Hills	0.56
InnerTerai	2.43
Terai	2.41

Source: Central Bureau of Statistics Sample Census of Agriculture, Nepal.

N.B. : The average size of cultivated holdings in the Hills is only a quarter of average in the *terai* area.

Productivity is higher in the *terai* than anywhere in Nepal outside the Kathmandu Valley. Prior to 1960 the *terai* was sparsely populated as a whole, largely as a result of the prevalence of malaria and other diseases; since that time, however, with effective malaria eradication and the dramatic reduction in cholera and smallpox, the terai has filled up rapidly with immigrants both from the Nepalese hills and from the densely populated Indian provinces to the south.

Current estimates suggest approximately 350,000 hectares of cultivatable land remaining to be exploited in the *terai* (sufficient to support directly roughly 156,000 households). If all of this land, however, were made available to immigrants from the hills it would take less than five years at the present rate of population growth to "fill up" completely, possibly as little as three years.

Elements of the Crisis

In 1971, twenty-five countries were identified by the U.N., on the basis of a number of economic and social indicators, as the "least-developed" in the world. Nepal was one of them, ranking somewhere within the bottom five and with a per capita income of less than $100 a year (IBRD 1973:3).

Most of these countries suffered, as does Nepal, from geographical isolation, poor internal communications and difficult terrain. Sixteen of the twenty-five, Nepal included, were land-locked. These in particular were generally dependent to an exceptional degree on relatively more developed neighbours for the transport of goods to and from the rest of the world, and were often, in addition, obliged to trade heavily with those neighbours from a position of weakness, for geographical, economic and political reasons, as in the case of Nepal with respect to India. Many of these countries were characterised not only by their extreme poverty, general lack of development and dependence on large and relatively powerful neighbours, but also by considerable internal inequalities in the spatial and social distribution of resources and of income. A significant number exhibited remarkably low levels of productive investment and a progressive deterioration of their general economic base, often obscured, as in the case of Nepal, by financial support' from outside the country and by excessively heavy use of crucial but limited physical resources within the country.

As recently as 1974, a U.N. report opened with the bleak statement: "...Nepal is poor and is daily becoming poorer" (ARTEP 1974). One authority on Nepal has written, of the period 1956-1965: "... the limited available economic data suggest that overall national output during this period grew at the average rate of about 2 per cent per annum, while population growth tallied about 2.5 per cent per year" (Beenhakker 1973:3). Despite the formal initiation of economic planning by central government in 1956, in the shape of a series of Five Year Plans, these have had little effect in stimulating significant growth in production per head.

Figures for the period 1961-1969, relating to the annual rate of growth in per capita food production - a crucial indicator in a country where nearly 95 per cent of the population are dependent on agriculture - suggest that, at best, Nepal attained a zero rate of growth during that decade. There is now good evidence to suggest that the Nepalese economy is having great difficulty even in keeping pace with population growth. (See Tables 3 and 4).

By the mid-1970s it had become painfully clear that the predominantly agrarian economy had hardly been able to keep pace with the increase in population, meeting requirements almost entirely through the cultivation of marginal land in the hills and the opening up of forest in the plains. The first of these had led to the development of large-scale erosion following the massive destruction of the forest cover while the second provided only a temporary safety valve for surplus population from the hills, although making possible a temporary substantial increase in food production and grain surplus in the plain (terai) regions.

The bulk of the population lives in the hills, and it is there that the crisis appears nearest. Already an area of food deficit for the most part, the hill regions are beginning to experience more frequent and more widespread food shortages, and overall declining per capita incomes. Even now the population in the hills is supported very largely by the export of labour outside Nepal and associated flow of remittances back to the remaining households; but as opportunities for temporary outside employment decrease - as there is evidence that they are - and local employment opportunities outside agriculture remain minimal, growing pressure will develop within the hill farming economy, which is likely to lead to a rapid diminution in the size of holdings (already, even in the early 1960s far smaller than in the terai) to increasing differentiation within the peasantry, both in terms of control over resources and in terms of income distribution, and to permanent emigration. Such emigration will, however, not solve the problem of extreme pressure on physical resources, for the emigrants form only a small proportion of the hill population and the dynamic of ecological collapse is very far advanced and will continue unless, at present levels of technology, population is substantially reduced. In 1971, at a conference on population and development, held in Kathmandu, one contributor observed that:

Table 3

GDP DISTRIBUTION BY SECTOR (IN MILLION Rs.)
(at Current Market Prices)

Sector	*1964/65*	*65/66*	*66/67*	*67/68*	*68/69*	*69/70*
Agriculture	3,915	4,694	4,218	5,217	5,890	6,563
Mining	1	2	1	1	1	1
Manufacturing	83	98	104	137	212	278
Construction	123	106	118	134	144	192
Transport, Communications & Services	91	93	102	120	141	168
Cottage Industry	392	469	462	522	589	656
Financial Institutions	69	80	82	87	106	128
Ownership of Dwellings	634	569	683	698	714	729
Public Administration and Defence	82	101	143	154	166	199
Public Utilities	4	5	8	10	11	15
Wholesale & Retail Trade	309	299	248	247	358	274
Services	170	177	204	219	235	256
Total	5,893	6,795	6,333	7,546	8,567	9,449

Source: Central Bureau of Statistics: Kathmandu

N.B.: GDP PER CAPITA in 1968/69 at 1964/65 Constant Prices: Rs 605 Annual rate of growth of GDP at 1964/65 Constant Prices: 2.7 per cent.

Table 4

POPULATION GROWTH RATE 1911-1976

Year	*Population*	*Year*	*Population*
1911	5,638,749	1952-4	8,473,478
1920	5,573,788	1961	9,799,820 (or 9,413,000)
1930	5,532,564	1971	11,556,000
1941	6,283,649	1976 (est.)	12,393,000

N.B.: Annual rate of growth 2.3 per cent

> "Visual evidence of already existing over-population includes deforestation, erosion and silting. Within the last decade, wooded hill-tops have been cut down or severely depleted, terraces have been extended to the tops of hills, and cattle have had to graze further away. In some areas, hill-top terraces have leached out, have been abandoned and have started to collapse on terraces below. Villagers often have to go much further to cut fodder for animals. The complex interaction of wood for fuel, cattle for manure and draught, and manured terraces for rice, etc., is becoming increasingly vulnerable to overcrowding of the Hill areas. If conditions worsen, areas now cultivated will have to be abandoned". (CEDA, 1971, 20).

The hope for the future is seen to lie with the demonstrated ability of the *terai* as a whole to produce substantial food grain surpluses and "industrial" crops, such as jute, sugar and mustard. On the basis of crop-production data provided by the Ministry of Agriculture and the Nepal Rastra Bank, it has been estimated that the terai's contribution to the nation's agricultural product is approximately 55 per cent. While over 70 per cent of industrial production takes place in the terai and some 65 per cent of all other economic activities contributing to the GDP (GDP = GNP minus Foreign Aid). (Gaige 1975:26).

Intensive settlement of the *terai* and the opening up of new land for cultivation there on a massive scale has only taken place within the last twenty years as the malaria eradication programme became effective and as population pressure in the hills built up to squeeze out significant numbers of hill farmers. There still remains a very substantial area of terai under forest, but official government policy has been to protect the forest as a source of timber for export and hence of revenue.[10] But this policy is coming under severe pressure as illegal tree-felling and settlement by immigrants both from the Nepalese hills and from the densely-populated Indian provinces across the border takes place on an increasing scale, and as timber contractors fail to meet their quotas on time. It might seem as if the elimination of the forests over much of the terai and their replacement by immigrant farmers would serve to postpone the crisis in the hills, and in the country as a whole, by acting as a "safety-valve". But such immigration from the hills is unlikely on its own to prevent their collapse and even the opening up of the entire terai to settlement would only postpone matters by up to five years. Furthermore, the certain loss of revenue would be considerable, and the returns from a mass of predominantly smallholders uncertain by comparison. Simply opening up the terai for uncontrolled settlement is not the answer.

The importance of the agricultural surplus, particularly the rice surplus, produced in the terai is very great; not only do the food deficit hill regions depend heavily on substantial rice imports from the terai, but the terai also exports large amounts to India. In 1965 an estimated 348,000 metric tons of rice were exported from Nepalese terai to India, making Nepal the fifth largest rice exporter in the world that year. Apart from rice, the terai produces surpluses of jute, tobacco, mustard oil seed, sugar cane, herbs, spices, timber, hides and many other agricultural commodities in smaller quantities. The Nepalese government levies duties on the export of agricultural commodities as well as on imported goods, and also on the processing of "industrial" crops; the terai thus contributes very significantly to government income.

The importance of the terai for the Nepalese economy, nd thus for the future of the nation as a whole, is undoubted. it unless productivity can be raised, in the terai even more crucially than in the hills, and unless measures are taken to encourage indigenous production and also to ensure that surpluses produced within Nepal do not merely leak out through illegal transactions across the Nepalese-Indian border, the hope that the terai offers for the future will prove illusory, and the existing surpluses will be eaten away by the growing population or the hill economy will collapse with all the economic and political consequences that that entails. The outlook is not promising for:

> "over the past decade, growth in aggregate output has been more or less neutralized by the population increases; moreover the rate of population growth appears to be accelerating. This poses a particularly difficult problem in the Hills, which have a limited resource base and which have long suffered from over-population. The slow pace of economic growth has taken place despite increasing public investment in agriculture and infrastructure. Slow growth of foodgrain production and rapid demographic growth have resulted in a rapid decline of the rice surpluses produced in the *terai* and exported to India, which finance a large part of Nepal's substantial import requirements. Foodgrain production in FY1972 has been far short of normal levels and the situation is critical in certain Hill areas. So far, the Government has procured about 150,000 tons of which 6,000 tons had to be airlifted." (IBRD 1973:3).

In this context the inadequacy of responses, both private and public, to the existing pressures and possibilities is both striking and disturbing. The majority of small and medium farmers, already heavily pressed by diminishing resources and low productivity, as well as by declining per capita incomes, find it hard to respond in an effective way. Only a tiny minority of these use chemical fertilizers and improved seed, and although there are signs of the development of a more intensive cropping pattern with increased multi-cropping during the year and even inter-cropping, the extent to which farming technology has altered over the past decade is limited. Water management, for example, which one might expect to show high returns in terms of improved yields for time and effort spent, seems remarkably unsophisticated in comparison with many other Asian countries. The cultivation of specific cash crops in the hills is limited. Even the larger landowners in the hills and in the terai, who might be expected to be increasing productivity and overall output, appear to be doing so marginally, if at all; and certainly the extent to which unambiguously capitalist' farming can be identified, even in the *terai*, remains limited.

The State's own efforts to increase agricultural productivity and to expand the range of cash crops grown remains largely ineffective, despite the establishment of such institutions as the Agricultural Development Bank to provide credit facilities and the creation of a "country-wide agricultural extension service" to provide advice and assistance particularly with new inputs. The use of chemical fertilizers and improved seeds *has* increased, but the aggregate effect to date of these new inputs has remained extremely limited, as has the service provided by the agricultural extension agents (JTA's = Junior Technical Assistants).

In the sphere of "industrial" production, Nepal is quite unable to compete with India and the ability of government to impose import control appears limited in the extreme.[11] Even the few traditional' forms of small-scale commodity production that survived in Nepal during the 19th and into the early 20th centuries have n ow collapsed in the face of competition from Indian manufacturers aided by scale economies and th protection of the Indian Government. The overwhelming superiority of Indian industrial capacity makes the establishment of industrial enterprises of any size fraught with difficulties and, without adequate protection, doomed to failure. The vast majority of manufacturing enterprises are very small, usually employing fewer than ten workers, or operating with family labour alone, and involving small capital investments in plant and equipment. The number of small industrialist' capitalists or petty commodity producers has undoubtedly increased, particularly in the terai, during the last decade, the most popular forms of enterprise being rice or oil mills, repair shops, hotels and restaurants and transport companies. It must be remembered, however, that industry contributes no more than about 10 per cent to Nepal's GDP and is thus of marginal significance, even today.

Very substantial numbers of individuals continue to move into commerce, usually as small retailers and most frequently to establish a supplementary source of income for a farm household. The balance of trade deficit ensures that the bulk of those in commerce are involved in trading imported manufactures. But in all, commerce involves little more than 3 per cent of the population and must also, therefore, like industry, be regarded as relatively insignificant, in comparison with agriculture, when considering the economy as a whole both past, present and future.

Unless major changes take place within Nepal to increase production, particularly in agriculture, and to ensure that the surpluses generated are productivity re-invested within the country, Nepal is threatened with a dangerously deepening crisis. The inadequate responses to date suggest that private individuals are incapable by virtue of their already precarious situation to make the rapid and radical change needed to cope with the coming crises. The insufficiency of the State's intervention to date requires further examination and explanation.

The statements made in the preceding paragraph cannot be fully substantiated here, although a fuller analysis is available from our other work (Blaikie, Cameron and Seddon, 1979; Blaikie, Cameron, Fleming and Seddon, 1977). It is important to bear in mind that these statements are not predictions of future events, but merely draw attention to the implications of existing trends for the immediate future.

Politics and the State

It is important to understand the nature of the Nepalese State in any except the most superficial, and limited (or single project') basic needs strategy for two reasons. First, the State includes institutions of government through which basic needs policies will be launched. These institutions are neither necessarily benign nor even neutral implementation agencies for policies designed to help the most vulnerable and deprived groups. Also they are not monolithic, and there will exist cleavages both between and within separate ministries, agencies, offices, etc. Thus there may well be conflicts of interest between different personnel in the face of a suggested basic needs policy. Secondly, the nature of the State itself determines the extent and form in which deprived and poor people can protect themselves against exploitation, and can develop their productive responses (both socially and physically) and thus themselves avail themselves of basic needs in an active manner.

Without an understanding of either the State or the institutions of government within it, the effect of any basic needs policy document will remain within the covers where it is written.

In the last twenty years there has undoubtedly been a massive expansion in the number of individuals employed directly by the State; this itself, has had major repercussions on the local economy and society in a number of districts. But the expansion of the bureaucracy cannot really be explained by a growing commitment to development. The notion of the State and the bureaucracy as being concerned primarily with bringing about economic and social development is a novel one in Nepal and one that breaks radically with the past. Historically the role of the State has been to maintain internal security and to appropriate sufficient of the surplus produced by farmers and others in the form of taxes, and sufficient of the profits made by traders, to maintain the State apparatus and the continued control of the ruling classes. Even today, after some twenty years of the rhetoric of democracy and development, there are clear indications that the definitive break with the past suggested by the use of such language has not taken place, and that the efforts of the State are still directed heavily towards raising revenues rather than stimulating production, and towards maintaining stability above all.

In Nepal today an aristocracy holds ultimate control of affairs of state and hence of formal politics. Involved heavily in the higher ranks of both the army and the administration, they are substantial landowners although some have invested in hotels, import-export business, tourist agencies and other commercial enterprises. The aristocracy is, in a sense, a section of a much larger ruling class of landowners.

In December 1960 the King, using the emergency powers given him by the Constitution, dissolved Parliament and the Cabinet, suspended the Constitution and banned all political parties. He publicly blamed the party-based parliamentary system of the previous decade for most of Nepal's difficulties and promised to restore to Nepal a more "suitable" form of democracy based on "the traditional practices of the Nepalese people". There was considerable unrest during the two years following this royal coup d'état and the now banned Nepali Congress Party, together with other parties opposed to the King's action, organised opposition both within Nepal and from across the border in India, despite the jailings of some of their leaders and many members. In 1962 the threat of a major war between India and China over the border led to a withdrawal of support for the exiles by the Indian government. The restoration of constitutional rights within Nepal, with the exception of the right to form political organisations, together with the withdrawal of Indian support, led to the collapse of overt organised opposition.

In the same year a new Constitution was drafted which created a four-tier system of *panchayats*, or councils, from the village, through district and zonal assemblies, to the national panchayat. The *panchayat* system provides in theory a pyramidal structure on a popular electoral base, at the apex of which is the National Assembly. Elections are held for the local *panchayat*, but the objectives of the system as a whole and its real significance are poorly understood.[12] No direct elections are held above the level of village and town *panchayat*, so the voting at the lower levels is confined almost entirely to local power considerations (see Gaige 1975:144-155). Despite the rhetoric of the *panchayat* system, with its Back to the Village' slogans reminiscent of China and Tanzania, there is little evidence of popular political involvement either in the *panchayats* themselves or in the class organisations', set up initially by the Government to represent such sectional interests as those of peasants, workers, women, ex-servicemen', but now effectively abolished.

At the top, decision-making level is the King, assisted by the Palace Secretariat.

> "During the past decade, the Crown has become the pivot around which the traditional interest groups, the sacred elite, the military, and the landowning aristocracy, still revolve. These groups gain access to the Royal Palace through their supporters and representatives on the staff of the Palace Secretariat. The Palace Secretariat has become the nerve-centre of administration and political structure in Nepal, even though its dominant policy and decision-making role is not defined via the law or within the Constitution of this country. The function of the Palace Secretariat can be closely compared with the previous, all-powerful function of the hereditary Rana Prime Minister's Office. That is, the Palace Secretariat today functions not only as a relay-station between King and the Government, but also as a decision-making component, frequently using the Central Government's Secretariat as an instrument for the implementation of decisions. This situation has led to a dual government' structure." (Beenhakker 1973:23).

Furthermore, the Council of Ministers, headed by the Prime Minister and Deputy Prime Minister, is directly nominated by the King from among the members of the National Assembly and the Ministers retain their positions only so long as they retain the confidence and approval of the King. The absence of a party-based political system, given the virtual lack of political involvement by the mass of the population, results in power remains formally within the bureaucracy and is concentrated at the top.

The upper echelons of the bureaucracy, particularly in central government and administration, derive overwhelmingly from the landowning classes, especially from the aristocracy; they also include a significant number of what might be termed traditional officials', predominantly of Brahmin and Chhetri caste, employed under the Ranas as civil servants but acting in effect as clients' of the aristocracy, and still in post despite the formal termination of Rana rule in 1951.

Distinct from these, and of increasing importance despite their relatively small numbers and uncertain position in the power structure, are what could best be termed modern bureaucrats', recruited from somewhat more diverse social backgrounds and having in common their relatively advanced education and technical expertise. Even if some of these, however, come from the middle class, the majority are the sons of landowners who have received their education at university in Kathmandu or abroad and who thus might be expected to have conflicting values and interests themselves. In general, however, they are committed to a greater extent than any other element within the ruling class and apparatus of state to the idea of economic (and hence inevitably to a certain extent of political) development in Nepal and will be more sympathetic to the necessary changes which we consider have to be made to fulfill basic needs strategy. This group might be expected to hold an increasingly influential position in government as the crisis in Nepal approaches and deepens, for their technical and organisational attributes give them powerful qualifications for coping with many of the economic, and even the political, problems that will inevitably develop over the next decade. For the present, however, it is still the fact that, all too often:

> "Instead of being valued for their specialised skills, they are often treated with contumely the politically appointed administrators and even more so by the administrators' transient bosses. In such a situation, the technical elites often find it necessary to devote attention to the complicated and fascinating game of intra-Secretariat

> politics, to the detriment of contributions in their fields of specialisation. Without the proper recognition and utilisation of the technical elites, however, it is inconceivable that any of the programs for the modernisation and industrialisation of Nepal can achieve any substantial success except for the few essentially symbolic industrial projects established by the various foreign aid programs." (Joshi & Rose 1966:517).

In its social and spatial structure, the bureaucracy reflects most of the inequalities prevalent in Nepalese society as a whole. But the perpetuation of privilege, patronage, discrimination, regional and ethnic inequality within the apparatus of state is damaging to Nepal's prospects because of the fact that, it is this essentially conservative apparatus that would have to conceive, plan and implement measures capable of preventing the coming crisis. So far, despite the existence of some men of high calibre and commitment in the higher reaches of the bureaucracy, the overwhelming tendency has been conservative and traditional' in the worst sense, and the effectiveness of state intervention limited. This is a fact which any basic needs strategy must confront.

The Economy and the State

In the next six paragraphs, a brief review of some policies and implementing agencies (all of which are relevant to a basic needs strategy and are taken up again in Chapter 4) is given as examples of the State's failure to intervene effectively in the production process. In an agrarian economy a prime area in which political and legislative changes can have dramatic effects on production and distribution is that of land tenure. During the early 1960's pressures were brought to bear on the government by foreign aid donors to implement some land reform and:

> "this message was not lost on the Nepalese Government. It needed to attract foreign aid and therefore it went through the motions of enacting land-reform legislation." (Gaige 1975:172).

The 1964 Land Act, however, did relatively little to alter the status quo. Firstly, the fact that such a large proportion of producers effectively owned their own land in any case meant that its proposals which never questioned the notion of private rights to land would have had a relatively limited effect, particularly in the hills where large landlords were rare. Secondly, the failure of the government to ensure adequate policing of the central elements of the legislation - which included the imposition of a land ceiling and the obligation to reduce holdings above this ceiling - meant that its total effect was extremely limited. By mid-1968, four years after its enactment, the Land Reform had produced only 146,000 acres for redistribution by the government and even by 1972 only 56,000 acres had actually been redistributed.

The government has recognised that major increases in agricultural production are required if the economy is not to collapse under the growing weight of its population. In the First Five Year Plan of 1956-1961, 31 per cent of the total budget was allocated to agriculture; in the Second Plan emphasis was placed on institutional reforms, including the attempt at Land Reform. In the Third Plan of 1966-1970, a major priority was again given to agricultural development, which was expected to produce an overall increase in foodgrain production of 15 per cent and in cash crops of 73 per cent. A review at the end of this period, however, showed that overall production of foodgrains was little more than 10 per cent above what it had been (despite significant increases in wheat and millet), while the increase in cash crop production was well below the anticipated figure. (See Tables 5 and 6).

> "The reasons for this shortfall in agricultural production are many. One is that the targets set were extremely ambitious when compared to available resources, both physical and human. Another reason is the lack of organised implementing machinery which created problems in proper co-ordination among the various projects." (Rana 1973:197).

Table 5

INDEX OF PHYSICAL OUTPUT OF VARIOUS CROPS, 1964/65-1969/70 (Base year 1964/65 = 100)

Crop	*1964/65*	*1965/66*	*1966/67*	*1967/68*	*1968/69*	*1969/70 (Preliminary estimates)*
Paddy	100.00	100.27	91.12	100.73	105.48	109.51
Maize	100.00	100.12	96.38	102.34	105.21	107.59
Wheat	100.00	116.66	126.19	150.79	180.16	191.75
Millet	100.00	190.49	190.49	176.45	175.70	184.34
Barley	100.00	107.69	107.69	100.00	110.48	112.86
Sugarcane	100.00	152.38	116.67	132.86	148.99	157.60
Oilseed	100.00	100.75	109.01	109.79	111.36	116.85
Potato	100.00	96.90	104.95	110.20	101.20	102.32
Tobacco	100.00	94.53	55.73	57.87	67.48	67.48
Jute	100.00	99.81	98.94	101.77	—	123.67

Source: Economic Analysis and Planning Division, Ministry of Food and Agriculture, HMB/Nepal, 1970.

Table 6

INDEX OF AGRICULTURAL PRODUCTION IN NEPAL, 1964/65-1969/70 (Base year 1964/65 = 100)

	1964/65	*1965/66*	*1966/67*	*1967/68*	*1968/69*	*1969/70*
Production	100.00	102.66	96.29	105.15	110.55	114.55

Source: Economic Analysis and Planning Division, Ministry of Agriculture, price used is wholesale for the year 1964/65.

Indeed, much can be laid at the door of inexperience - after all Nepal had no economic planning of any kind prior to 1951 - and certainly of considerable importance is the serious lack of trained personnel at all levels, particularly in what is referred to as middle level manpower' (including fieldworkers in health and agricultural extension) where wages are low, promotion prospects poor and back-up in terms both of technical advice and of material assistance seriously defective. Given such a situation, even if there were a general commitment on the part of the ruling classes and top bureaucrats to developing the national economy as a whole the lack of trained personnel and poor coordination within the bureaucracy would ensure a low level of success in devising and carrying out effective development projects within an overall planning framework. Crucial however, to understanding the failure of State intervention and planning is recognition of the fact that such a commitment does not exist despite ministerial speeches, public proclamations and at least verbal encouragement from the Palace itself.

Within agriculture, the government has, since 1960, set up organisations for education and research, horticulture, livestock, fisheries and agricultural extension; the Agricultural Extension Department has posted a District Agricultural Development Officer (DADO) in many districts and a varying number of Junior Technical Assistants (JTAs) in each district.

Yet:

> "extension services do not seem to have produced any significant results, particularly in the hill districts. The foremost reason for this is not only that the number of JTAs is few, but they are also inadequately trained and have little relevant experience to extend to the farmers." (Rana 1973:198).

The Agricultural Development Bank was established in 1960 to provide loans for the purchase of fertiliser, seeds and insecticides. The impact of the ADB has been limited, however, by the fact that not only are funds inadequate to met credit needs but a real difficulty is created by the large amount of land or other assets normally required as collateral to qualify for credit; this ensures that credit is limited largely to those already relatively well-off. The Agricultural Supply Corporation, formed in 1966, also distributes improved seeds, fertiliser and farm implements. By 1969 this corporation had distributed over 12,000 tons of fertiliser and 1,500 tons of improved seed through 44 co-operatives and 215 private dealers.

Even so, these amounts are relatively small and more is required to maintain overall output and yields let alone increase them significantly. (See Table 7).

Despite these various efforts the Fourth Five Year Plan (1970-1975) recognised that; "although a number of developmental works have been undertaken in different sectors of the economy, there has not been virtually any noteworthy change in the basic condition of agriculture" (National Planning Commission 1970:5) and what change has occurred has been limited both spatially and socially. Indeed a recent article written by a member of the Planning Commission, in the journal *Pragya*, recognises that:

Table 7
YIELD TRENDS OF VARIOUS CROPS, 1961/1965 - 68 (K/hectare)

Crop	*1961/62*	*1965/66*	*1966/67*	*1967/68*	*Percentage change in 1967/68 over 1961/62*
Paddy	2010	1968.4	2006.3	1961.9	-2.39
Maize	1967	1902.2	1831.1	2016.1	+2.48
Wheat	946	1483.0	1496.0	1266.6	+31.39
Millet	1312	1200.0	1200.0	1200.0	-8.54
Sugarcane	19886	14769.2	14700.0	15218.5	-23.47
Jute	1236	1209.3	1200.0	1067.2	-13.63
Mustard	553	529.9	573.1	595.1	+7.60
Potato	6628	6595.2	6976.7	7325.5	+10.52
Tobacco	830	1100.0	650.0	675.0	-18.61

Source: Ministry of Economic Planning, Central Bureau of Statistics, National Sample Census of Agriculture, Yield Data of Principle Crops, 1961 (Kathmandu: HMG 1965), pp.6,11; And U.S. AID/Nepal, Program Office, Economic Planning Section, Economic Data Papers - Nepal, II:1 (Kathmandu, August 1969), p.37.

> "The major part of the achievements of process of development in Nepal have been confined to Kathmandu Valley, some areas of East and Central Terai, Hetauda, Pokhara, Butwal, and Bhairahawa. Even in these areas, the majority of the population has not benefited. The fruits of development have been achieved mainly by big and middle class businessmen, landowners, contractors for construction and supply, some intelligentsia in certain technical and administrative fields, doctors, lawyers, some opportunist journalists and auditors, owners of hotels and restaurants and those administrators who have helped these in private sector and the affluent to evade regulations and the law."

Conclusion

We maintain that Nepal today is in crisis: a crisis associated with the particular form of relations of production (and thus class relations), with the failure of any social class to develop the productive forces sufficiently to provide the necessary expansion of the economic base to support a rapidly growing population, and with the particular form of the contemporary State. Elements of that crisis, in manifest form, include *growing food shortages; environmental deterioration;* and *unemployment,* resulting from the structural underdevelopment of the agrarian economy; the extension of rather than the intensification of cultivation; rapid population growth; and from the virtual absence of employment opportunities outside agriculture. Associated with these manifest elements of the crisis are major *spatial and social inequalities* in terms of access both to resources for production and to facilities for consumption. For the vast majority of peasants and workers in Nepal the crisis which reflects the structural underdevelopment of the economy is persistent and chronic; the reproduction of deprivation and poverty, which is a function of the continuing underdevelopment of Nepal, manifests itself nationally as a crisis, and for the vast majority of the rural and urban population as constant hardship, uncertainty and desperation.

Given the social deprivation and material poverty associated for the mass of the population with the crisis in Nepal, it is clear that a development strategy of the basic needs kind is required.

NOTES

8. Agriculture contributes some 67 per cent to Nepalese GDP, 15 per cent of which comes from livestock production and 52 per cent from production of crops.

9. A recent World Bank Report observes, of the hills, that "...population density per sq.km of arable land is probably as high as 1,100, a concentration similar to that found in certain Asiatic deltas, but where, in contrast, the soil is more fertile and the climate allows two or three crops a year." (IBRD 1873:4).

10. Gaige points out that:

    "....because Nepal's most valuable stands of timber are located in *terai* districts and because roads are available to transport the timber to Indian markets, 87 per cent of timber revenue comes from this region. Of the remaining timber revenue, the inner *terai* valleys produce 9 percent and the western hills 4 per cent". (Gaige 1975:27-28).

11. Largely by virtue of the Trade and Transit treaties with India, themselves imposed upon Nepal as a small land-locked mountain state dominated by a large and powerful neighbour.
12. This is shown by a survey reporting that in a number of selected panchayats roughly 50 per cent of those interviewed said that they were 'deeply confused' about the panchayat system, while a further 40 per cent had either a 'rudimentary knowledge' or expressed 'incomprehension'. (Shrestha & Mohsin 1970:80).

2
WEST CENTRAL NEPAL

Location and Timing of Fieldwork

The fieldwork component on which this report rests was carried out during 1974/75 and in Spring 1978. Prior to the OECD project, we had already spent four man years in Nepal carrying out an evaluation on the impact of road construction in West Central Nepal for the United Kingdom Ministry of Overseas Development, and a further four man years analysing and writing up the material collected in the field. During the course of this ODM project, a rural survey was conducted (the sampling design and content of which are described below in 3) which provided the basis for a resurvey of some selected households in Spring 1978 specifically for this report. All the fieldwork for both studies was undertaken in the west central region of Nepal (see Figure 1), and it remains to provide a general contextual account of this region into which an analysis of basic needs requirements can be placed.

West Central Nepal - General Characteristics

This region is designated as the West Central Planning Region, with the town of Pokhara as its headquarters. According to the 1971 census, West Central Nepal had a population of some 2,500,000 and a total land area of approximately 34,000 square kilometres. Just over 10 per cent of this area was cultivated and overall population density per cultivated hectare was just under 7. There is considerable variation in population density from sub-region to sub-region, however, the plains (*terai*) being still relatively sparsely populated with 3 to the cultivated hectare, the northern mountain areas with between 6 and 7, and the hills having as high a population density per cultivated hectare as between 10 and 15.

The region is divided into three administrative zones: Dhaulaghiri in the north, consisting almost entirely of mountainous terrain (which was not sampled in the surveys); Gandaki, in the middle, consisting of hills and valleys; and Lumbini, in the south, including both hills and the terai, the latter two zones containing over 90 per cent of the total population of the region.

In terms of travel time the region is larger than Western Europe - meaning that it takes as long, even after the building of motorable roads, to travel from one extremity of the region to the other by the fastest means of ground transport available as it does to travel from northern Finland to southern Greece by rail or road. This had strong implications for sampling and research design.

Gandaki Zone covers approximately that part of the study area called "the inner hills" (that is, excluding a strip of outer hills which fall into the Lumbini Zone to the south). Altitudes range from about 800 metres in the deepest valley floor to 3,500 metres on the top of the highest Himalayan foothills. There is a high population density per cultivated hectare, considering yields are very low compared with the *terai* (a density of about 12 persons per cultivated hectare, varying from 7 in the north to 14.3 in the west). The major crops are paddy, cultivated on the *khet* (irrigated) fields, and maize and millet on the *pakho* (upland, dry) fields, although wheat on *khet* land is being introduced in some limited areas. Fruit trees (apricot, oranges, tangerines, lemons and limes, and bananas in the deep valleys) provide some cash income and

WEST CENTRAL PLANNING REGION - NEPAL

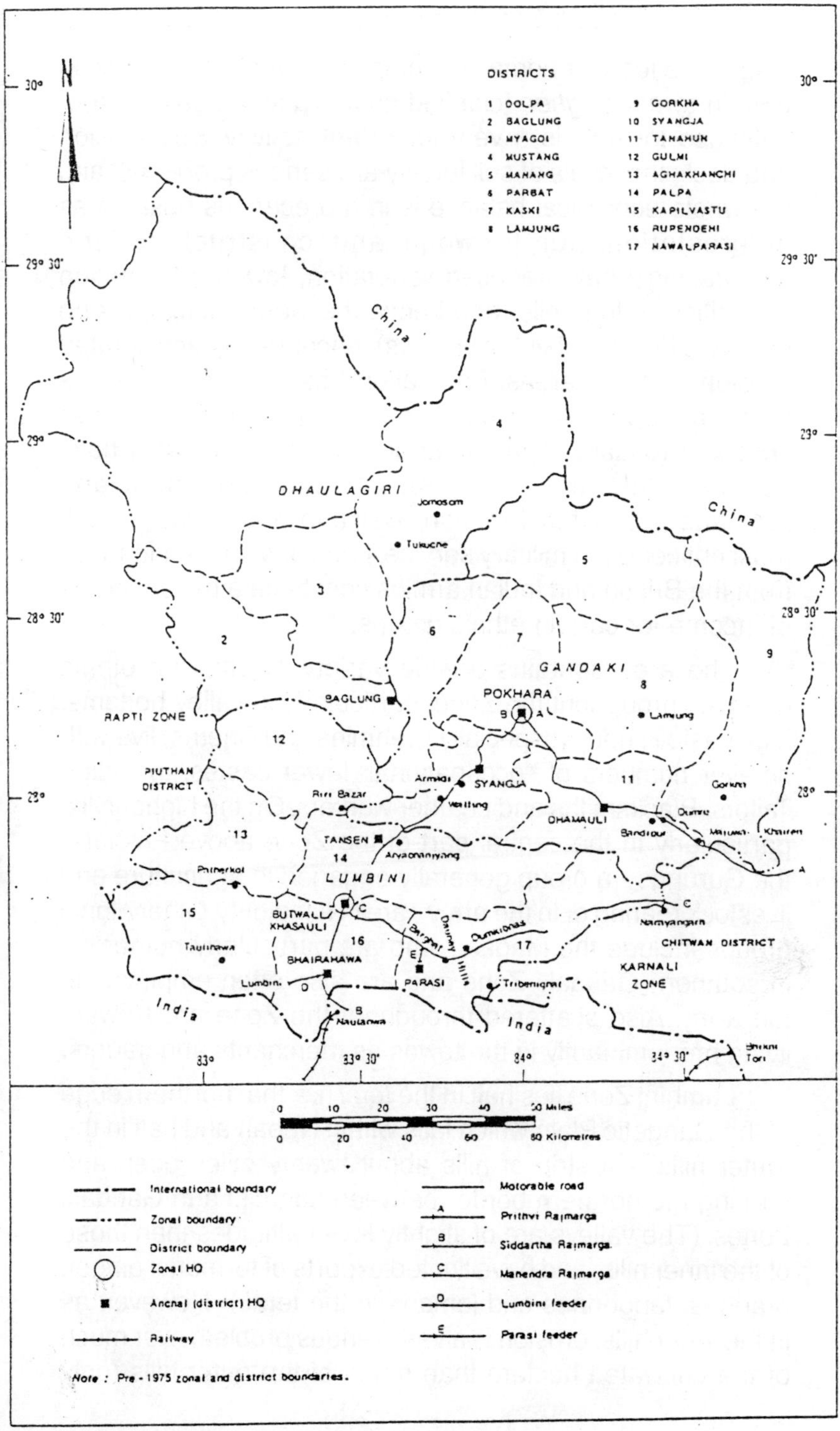

also some food for home consumption. Livestock production both in terms of *ghee* (clarified butter) and the sale of she-buffaloes for milk is a very important activity. Soil erosion and declining levels of soil fertility are serious problems, and the whole ecological balance is in a precarious position as deforestation (for firewood and construction) and overgrazing[13] have reduced vegetation, lowered infiltration capacities of the soils (and hence the water table, causing special difficulty in hill-top villages), encouraging accelerated erosion in many areas. Emigration has been and still is a frequent response to declining living standards, either seasonal (usually to the *terai* or India both of which have seasonal labour shortages), or semi-permanent and permanent, to Uttar Pradesh, Calcutta and further afield, most noticeably in military service. Pensions and remittances from the British and Indian armies constitute a major source of income for certain ethnic groups.

The area contains a wide variety of different ethnic groups. Throughout the Zone, particularly in valley bottoms, high caste Hindus (especially Brahmins and Chetris) live with smaller numbers of "occupational" lower castes, including Tailors, Blacksmiths and Leather workers. On the higher hills, particularly in the central part of the Zone above Pokhara, the Gurungs - a group generally engaged in agriculture and livestock rearing or in the army - are in a majority. Other ethnic groups include the Magars, who are particularly numerous in southern Gandaki Zone and are also often employed in the army. Also scattered throughout the Zone are Newars living predominantly in the towns as merchants and traders.

Lumbini Zone lies half in the *terai* (i.e. that northern edge of the Gangetic Plain which falls within Nepal) and half in the "outer hills" - a strip of hills about twenty miles deep and forming the northern border between Lumbini and Gandaki Zones. (The valleys are of slightly lower altitudes than those of the inner hills, and have limited exports of turmeric, ginger, oranges, tangerines and lemons to the terai.) However, as in the inner hills, erosion is a very serious problem over much of the cultivated hectare than much of the outer hills (only

2.8). In terms of the percentage of the population of the study area living in the terai, official statistics may be misleading because of illegal settlement from India and from the hills, not included in the census enumeration. Part of the *terai* immediately abutting on to the hills is heavily forested, although commercial lumbering and illegal settlement is reducing the forested area rapidly. To the south of the forest belt where the trees have been cleared in the more distant past, paddy cultivation in *khet* (irrigated) fields, with mustard and winter wheat are widespread. Both from observation and secondary sources, most of the terai in the study area can be designated a cereal surplus area which exports both illegally and legally to India and also to the hills to the north. Bhairahawa (now Siddarthanager) is the major cereal market for the area.

Each of these Zones is in turn divided, for administrative and political purposes, into Districts (or, in Nepali, *Zilla*). There are 17 in the study area with populations varying from 7,000 in the sparsely populated north to 262,000 in the outer hills. Their areas vary from 6,208 sq. kms (again in the north), to 1,098 sq.kms. Modal values for both these statistics are 130,000 persons, and 1,600 sq.kms. Many districts are conspicuously heterogenous (e.g. Gorkha District which ranges from the Tibetan border with peaks of 8,000 metres to valleys of 650 metres in the south). Figure 1 shows the location and names of all the Districts in Gandaki and Lumbini Zones.

Each District is in turn divided into about fifty to ninety *gaon* (village *panchayats* and each of these into nine wards (consisting of between 7 and 150 households). Considerable heterogeneity often exists within village *panchayats*, particularly of altitude, aspect (with profound effects on cropping patterns) and in ethnic composition. The ward itself is usually less heterogenous and was found by us to provide a convenient sampling unit for the surveys of household consumption and farm production.

Thus the study area covers one Planning Region, which is divided successively into three Zones, 17 Districts and about 1,400 village *panchayats*, each with nine wards. Since considerable variation is found in terms of physical characteristics such as altitude and aspect, which may have profound effects on agricultural production and socio-economic characteristics, adequate aggregation and sampling required information on *panchayats,* which the administration could not provide. Below the District level, information on the localities is sparse, even the voters lists within village *panchayats* for example are often inaccurate or out-dated. The tenuous nature of the administration's information on much of the rural area is indicated by the inaccuracy of maps and ignorance of even the general location of village *panchayats* in several District headquarters.

The Rural Survey of 1974/75, and the Sample for the "Basic Needs" Study

The 1974/75 Survey was administered by small teams of Nepalese workers, almost always accompanied by one of the present authors of this report. The data are of an unusually high standard since checking of the questionnaire (including quantitative tests of household budget balances) was done locally and follow-up visits made if necessary. The sampling design was a multi-level stratified one in which five Districts were chosen from seventeen on the basis of a Mahanalobis D^2 test; from these wards were selected from each District and once selected were identified by the village within which they were situated. Thus each of the nine wards in every village *panchayat* was included in a set for each selected District as the total population from which sample wards were to be chosen. Forty-five wards in total were randomly chosen, and a random 25 per cent sample of households was drawn from the updated electoral register for each of these wards. This procedure gave a sample of 667 households. The questionnaire gathered information upon production and consumption, a wide range of social, economic and political relations between members of the households, other households, the bureaucracy and other institutions (for the contents of the questionnaire itself see Blaikie, Cameron, Fleming and Seddon, 1976, 9: 1-9:46).

The information was coded, checked and put on tape, and had already been tried in a number of analyses before our revisit for the Basic Needs Study in Spring 1978. (See Blaikie, Cameron, Seddon and Fleming, 1977).

In order to select households for re-interview in 1978 we extracted from this rural survey information on all households deriving more than half their foodgrains from labouring off their own farm. This criterion was used not only because such households generally had low consumption levels in all spheres but also because of the considerable social disadvantages such households have. Thus we could ensure that the major elements of basic needs deficiency would be represented in our sample. This gave us a core for our sample over 100 households on which we possessed complete information regarding economic activity and consumption three years previously. We took a print-out of the data on each household to the field for the re-interviews to provide an on-the-spot check on changes since 1974/75, and to help us to approach the re-interview with a freshly rehearsed background knowledge of the interviewee. Also we took to Nepal the data we had collected on urban poor and lower-paid workers who had been interviewed in our previous studies. The 77 rural households finally interviewed were in a sub-sample of 13 locations chosen as representing a variety of conditions with respect to communications, population concentration and topography within a feasible overall travel plan. However it must be emphasized that basic needs deficiencies are not only to be found in the group identified here - even if a "technical" and inadequate conception of basic needs as a minimum consumption level is taken. There are large numbers of rural households who derive more than half their foodgrains from their farm who are desperately poor also.

Interviews with individuals and households were informal but structured so as to cover the areas investigated three years ago and then to lead into open-ended discussion of "basic needs", actions households had taken to achieve these needs, and the outcomes of these actions. Wherever feasible, several members of the household were involved but participation of people from outside the household was discouraged, especially excluding outsiders and neighbours where patron-client relationships were likely to interfere with householders' responses. Statements about events were corroborated from several "independent" interviews but the problem of preserving anonymity of sources did restrict active pursuit into official records of disputes and conflicts. Interviews often lasted for over two hours and sufficient time was spent in each location to allow re-visits if necessary. Failure to identify selected households was very rare and no household refused to be interviewed.

The Vulnerable Groups in West Central Nepal

In order to place the vulnerable groups which we re-visited in 1978 in the context of all groups of rural society, we have included a table (Table 8) which provides a quantitative summary of the social and economic relationships in which the households surveyed were involved in 1974/75, and also an indication of the proportion of households we consider particularly vulnerable to a general deficiency of "basic needs".

The households of the survey are classified in Table 8 principally by their control over the means of production and by the importance of their involvement in the market. We considered that both control over production and the level of production were the most important criteria determining the fulfilment of basic needs. The columns represent the social position of the household in the production process: labourers (columns 1 and 2) where the control over production is minimal; households that do possess land over which they have control but are obliged to work for others for some of (but less than half of) their total foodgrain requirement (columns 3 and 4); domestic producers who do not significantly employ others nor are obliged to be employed by others (columns 5 and 6); employers who have sufficient means of production to employ others (columns 7-10). In the last columns are households with opportunities for

Table 8

NUMBERS AND PERCENTAGES OF RURAL SURVEY INTERVIEWING CROSS-TABULATED BY TOTAL CASH FARM SALES, RELATIONS IN EMPLOYMENT AND EXISTENCE OF NON-AGRICULTURAL INCOME

"Class" position of households	Labourers: (greater than 1/2 food grain not from own farm)		Labours+Dom./Peasant producers: (at least Rs. 200 from llab. butess than 1/2 food grain)		Dom./Peasant Producers:not more than Rs. 200 given/ received for labouring)		Small Employers/Rich Peasants (Rs.200 — Rs. 1000 paid to labourers)		Large Employers/(Feudal & Capitalist): (more than Rs. 1000 paid for labouring)		Row	
	Col.1	2	3	4	5	6	7	8	9	10		
Non-agricultural income / Income from farm sales in a year	With	Without	With	Without	With	Without	With	Without	With	Without	Total	%
A. < Rs. 250	44	68	24	39	108	12	9	1	6	0	311	46.9%
B. Rs.250-499	2	5	9	15	26	10	3	1	0	0	71	10.6%
C. Rs.500-749	0	7	2	8	14	12	3	1	1	0	48	7.2%
D. Rs.750-999	0	4	0	7	16	21	4	4	4	0	56	8.4%
E. Rs.1000-1999	0	5	3	7	19	29	7	7	3	1	83	12.4%
F. Rs. 2000-4999	0	1	0	5	8	17	9	20	4	9	73	10.9%
G.Rs. 5000	0	0	0	0	0	2	4	4	4	11	25	3.7%
Column Total	48	90	38	81	191	103	39	38	18	21	667	100.0%
	7.2	13.5	5.7	12.1	28.6	15.4	5.8	5.7	2.7	33.3		

N.B. Rounding procedures have produced some minor discrepancies in % figures; *Source:* Rural Survey 1975 Categories of households from which 1978 resurvey was sampled.

significant accumulation (e.g. columns 9 and 10). These categories of household are further subdivided into those who *have* and those who *have not* non-agricultural income. Since employment in the army or the bureaucracy or in some menial capacity in India (as household servants, guards etc.) is an important element in "propping up" the ailing agricultural economy, its existence can considerably improve a household's position, or at least qualify the negative implications of its lack of control of production. The rows represent the size of surpluses from the farm sold in the market, and are good indicators of a household's ability to accumulate (since taxation is low), and its vulnerability to malnutrition and unforeseen setbacks.

The first and second columns from the left constitute those 112 of the sampled households whose basic needs deficiency are undoubtedly greatest in all dimensions. The interviews for the revisit in 1978 were primarily drawn from the two cells shown surrounded by heavy lines. However it must be emphasized again that basic needs deficiencies are to be found frequently outside both these two cells. Amongst the households in the two first columns (including the sub-set from which the revisit sample was drawn) are the following types:

1. vulnerable domestic producers of a generation or more ago, now unable to even meet half of their grain requirements from their own land (due to, say, a distress sale of land or landslips) often compounded by the inability to find alternative sources of income due to caste prejudice;
2. displaced occupational; castes unable any longer to earn a livelihood from craft occupations within the domestic form of production (see, for a case study example section 6.c);
3. immigrants from India and other parts of Nepal working as labourers and hoping to earn enough by their labour (and financial support from relatives in India or patrons in Nepal) to buy some land; and
4. households whose history of slave and/or bonded labour goes back several generations.

Labouring households with non-agricultural income and/ or with some sales of farm produce suffer no worse hardships in consumption terms than many of those with more land but no outside income. However, chronic poverty found in survey data was confirmed by the in-depth interviews. A period of severe under-nourishment just before the harvesting of the maize crop and more general malnutrition throughout the year were frequently reported.

Information on consumption was collected from all households in the rural survey as part of the questionnaire. A check on the responses was made through comparing cash and food-grain incomes and outgoings on a balance sheet constructed after the interview, but even so the figure can only be indicators of a general order of magnitude of consumption levels. The amounts of basic foodstuffs consumer per capita organised for 19 groups are shown in Table 9. This table shows labourers in general as among the most malnourished, consuming relatively large amounts of cheap spices (especially chilli) in order to ease the hunger of insufficient and otherwise monotonous food. Leaving aside the debate upon minimum dietary requirements as an objective criterion for nutritional adequacy, we compared the consumption of the least fortunate labourers'group (without outside income and marketing less than Rs.250 worth of produce in a year) with a "control" group: "domestic" producers (without outside income and marketing more than Rs.500 worth of produce a year), assuming activity levels are similar. This shows that consumption of milk, *ghee*, pulses and meat (the major sources of protein) is much more than double for the group with relatively unconstrained access to food resources. Also a substitute of millet for rice is clearly discernible for these groups.

The vital distinction is that the social relationships in which labourers are involved impose not only immediate material poverty, but an absence of control over the situation in which poverty is deepened on a day-to-day and generation-to-generation basis. As ecological decline and division of land through inheritance continues, it is inevitable that increasing numbers of households are forced on to the labour market in conditions which leave them vulnerable to malnutrition as well as to temporary disabilities and illness, leading to debt and subsequent sale of their few remaining assets. At the time of survey in 1974/5, 28.6 per cent of all households interviewed had income from outside agriculture, often critical in maintaining their positions in the "domestic" category.

The close relationship between great poverty and labouring for others suggested that further studies should be undertaken in the rural areas to investigate the relationships which labourers have with employers. In general we found in the survey that the relations between wage labourer and employer were very varied. However, there are three distinct types. The first is between the labourer and a farm household which requires a small amount of non-family labour every year. Many of the advantaged small farmers (and even a few with smaller resource bases) hire up to the equivalent of Rs.200 of labour a year, usually for ploughing and harvesting. The availability of work for the labourer will depend upon non-market, personal relations between employee and employer. The second type occurs between larger employers of labour and casual labourers, where the employer, after selecting employees from local sources, will then make up any shortage from migrant labour (although this latter characteristic is limited to the terai - the hills' labour markets are normally saturated by local labour). Thirdly, a labourer may contract to become a "permanent labourer" (haruwa) for a minimum period of a year (the contract can only be annulled if there is substantial cause for complaint by either party). The relationship between employer and employee in this case is reinforced by the status and power of the employer with respect to all aspects of the employee's life.

We also instituted a number of studies to investigate the position of labourers in towns (not included in Tables 8 and 9). This involved looking particularly at lower-paid workers, whose jobs represented the most immediately available opportunity for those unable to earn a living in the rural areas. The findings of these studies highlighted the rudimentary

Table 9

AVERAGE PER CAPITA CONSUMPTION PER WEEK OF BASIC FOODS AND COMMODITIES IN KG.

Position in ag.	Wage Labouring				Domestic				Large Employees		
Non ag. income	Without		With		Without		With		Without	With	
Farm Sales (Rs.)	<250	>250	<250	>250	<500	>500	<500	>500	>1000	<1000	>1000
Rice	1.756	2.749	1.459	1.581	2.372	1.928	1.094	1.521	2.696	2.042	2.097
Millet	0.547	0.340	0.969	0.360	0.723	0.329	1.109	0.954	—	0.192	—
Maize	0.498	0.228	0.429	0.492	0.491	0.436	0.981	0.714	—	0.496	0.050
Wheat	0.192	0.604	0.179	0.639	0.334	0.249	0.278	0.389	0.971	0.340	0.864
Potatoes	0.189	0.179	0.134	0.133	0.229	0.231	0.340	0.372	0.490	0.241	0.139
Pulse	0.140	0.135	0.124	0.271	0.293	0.417	0.166	0.204	0.379	0.182	0.241
Vegetables	0.321	0.282	0.371	0.174	0.590	0.382	0.219	0.246	0.287	0.420	0.365
Dry Vegetables	—	0.010	0.021	—	—	0.010	0.023	0.025	—	—	—
Milk (litres)	0.181	0.304	0.230	0.469	0.374	0.556	0.607	0.522	0.604	2.087	0.994
Meat	0.009	0.008	0.027	0.002	0.024	0.018	0.019	0.040	0.034	0.101	0.047
Fish	0.023	—	0.002	—	—	0.004	—	—	0.020	—	0.011
Ghee	0.008	0.015	0.015	0.009	0.041	0.028	0.032	0.030	0.037	0.068	0.027
Cooking Oil	0.045	0.043	0.057	0.145	0.079	0.049	0.033	0.049	0.134	0.062	0.050
Salt	0.128	0.172	0.128	0.190	0.220	0.176	0.133	0.130	0.214	0.111	0.144
Spices	0.062	0.066	0.073	0.077	0.086	0.057	0.065	0.070	0.088	0.057	0.060
Sugar	0.017	0.022	0.039	0.050	0.024	0.057	0.050	0.110	0.064	0.179	0.097
Molasses	0.010	0.028	0.008	0.019	0.044	0.014	0.010	0.008	0.053	—	—
No.of cases	68	22	44	44	22	22	134	57	21	7	11
Average Family Size	5.299	6.318	5.091	5.250	2.727	6.259	5.933	6.930	6.429	7.8000	10.273

Source : Rural Survey 1975

Categories of households from which 1978 resurvey was drawn

nature of urban development in West Central Nepal and especially the very limited opportunities for rural migrants. It was clear however that daily wages in urban employment tend to be higher than in agriculture. Depsite this, although work in the towns is often regarded as an attractive short-term proposition it is rare for urban workers to remain long in one job. This is particularly true of the lower-paid workers. For instance a survey of lower-paid workers (i.e. those earning less than 200 rupees a month) carried out during 1974 in the three largest towns, showed that roughly half the completed jobs held by interviewees had lasted for less than two years (in Pokhara 60 per cent lasted less than two years, in Butwal 48 per cent and in Bhairahawa 45 per cent). There are various reasons for this on the side of the employee. One is that urban employment is usually seen as an additional rather than the only source of income for a family. Virtually all of those in employment in the towns, whether in casual low-paid labouring jobs or in more secure higher-paid clerical or managerial posts have access to farming land, either through personal ownership or through their relatives, and thus do not depend solely on urban wages for their livelihood. Roughly 75 per cent of the lower-paid workers interviewed in Butwal, for example, owned some land. Work in the towns, under these circumstances, tends to assume for the less well-off, the form of a "target" employment, in which an individual aims to earn a particular amount, in many cases for a particular purpose over a given - and usually quite short - period. In addition to this, the labour demands of the family farm are often responsible for drawing an individual in urban employment back to the countryside within a relatively short period.

In those cases where a worker's family appeared to be relatively well-off and thus able to employ wage labour themselves on the farm, the urban worker was generally concerned with questions of personal pride and social status back in the village rather than purely financial consideration. A few of those in urban employment in the larger towns were younger men who had left home to try to join the army, and, failing that, had decided to earn something before returning home, so as to appear (in the words of one such man).... "able to make good outside the protection of the village". It is significant in this regard that those interviewed in the lower-paid workers' survey tended to be young men; in Butwal, 65 per cent of those interviewed were between 16 and 30, in Bhairahawa 74 per cent were in this age range, while in Pokhara the proportion was 90 per cent. Some of those in urban employment above the age of 30 expressed concern that they should soon return to look after their own land on a permanent basis rather than continue to work away from home.

Another reason for leaving a job after a relatively short period is that working conditions are often bad, particularly for those in menial jobs. Reasons given for dissatisfaction with a job included low pay, physically hard work, unpleasant work, no leisure time and poor relations with the employer. Given the fundamentally casual basis of most low paid employment and the maintenance by urban workers of strong ties with the rural economy, dissatisfaction tends to be expressed first in grumbling and then in quitting employment rather than collective organised action. The very limited employment opportunities outside agriculture thus produce responses in employees which produce the image of an uncommitted labour force which, in turn, provides a reason for non-productive investment by private individuals and the State.

Although it was found that in the urban areas as a whole the majority of employees earn less than 200 rupees a month, there were variations from town to town, and differences between sectors. For example, employees in the catering and hotel business (including hotels, restaurants, bhattis and tea shops) were generally paid low wages even in comparison with the lowest paid in other sectors.There was also evidence to suggest that, in general, wages paid in what could be identified as "modern" establishments, including the larger "factories" orproduction units, motor workshops and bus companies (where technical skills were important) were higher than the average elsewhere. Dividing business establishments into three major "sectors" (industrial, commercial and service) this broad distinction becomes clear (see Table 10).

Table 10

PROPOSITION OF LABOURERS BY WAGE RANGE IN SECTORS

Wage Range (Rs. per month)	*Industrial*	*Commercial*	*Service*
1-200	49.2%	51.5%	67.1%
201-400	38.2%	46.0%	27.1%
400 +	12.6%	2.4%	5.6%

Source: Urban Workers' Survey 1974.

Food and lodging form an integral part of "payment" in virtually all lower-paid employment and highly personalised relations develop which bind the employee to his employer - this is particularly true in the restaurant and hotel business. Indeed, investigations showed that approximately 50 per cent of jobs are obtained through some previous connection between employer and employee, involving some form of kinship or neighbourly relationship in town, or more usually, back in the village. It is significant that it is in the largest centres of employment, where the larger establishments are to be found - i.e. in Butwal and Bhairahawa - that lower-paid workers tend to be older and to stay longer in any particular job. Only in Bhairahawa at the Sugar Mill (employing 600 individuals in the peak period) was found full collective action by employees to improve working conditions and raise wages.

The situation of both the rural and urban deprived described here contrasts sharply with the ideology of the independent free-holding peasant which is prevalent in many planning documents, and in the current conventional wisdom of much rural development planning. The strength of this ideology has contributed to the condition of agricultural labourers or sub-marginal peasants being in an important sense invisible. This "invisibility" is rooted in two relationships which derive from national and international factors, and thus must be included in analysis at the level of the nation-state. The first is the absence of any direct access to the central authorities through present systems of political and legal representation, thus de facto leaving rural labourers unenfranchised. Secondly migration to India (avoiding the spatially intervening opportunity of Nepalese towns) has produced a much smaller local urban poverty problem than the general situation of rural development would warrant.

But invisibility from above does not necessarily mean passivity below and the OECD "basic needs" project allowed us to return to Nepal in 1978 to examine in more detail the implications of the crisis in Nepal for the m most vulnerable. Our previous work suggested a conflict between the most vulnerable (who are economically vital, but excluded from control over resources and officially invisible), who were experiencing continuos hunger and were faced with unpromising migration as the only legitimate alternative - and those in positions of power over them (whether as direct employers or as those in the higher ranks of government). Our aim in the recent fieldwork was to investigate the forms that this conflict was taking and to attempt to understand the deprived as active subjects in relationships not of their choosing, rather than passive victims of inevitable processes. The new investigations were however firmly based on the groundwork provided by our previous collective four years of fieldwork in the study area.

Methodology of Resurvey and a "Basic Needs" Approach

Our perspective of a basic needs strategy demanded a reconsideration of methodology. Previously much of our work was based on questionnaire surveys and official reports. A basic needs approach implies a specific methodology which involves greater emphasis on understanding the actions of the deprived themselves (e.g. in-depth interviewing and oral histories). Obviously any complete study must involve elements of both qualitative and quantitative approaches but the emphasis on the former is important. An approach to basic needs which too exclusively uses a "top-down/macro" methodology will have great trouble in avoiding reducing "basic needs" to a measurement-identification-delivery adjunct to some other development strategy. Similarly the "bottom-up/macro" emphasis that we adopted cannot avoid taking full cognisance of political implications, even those uncomfortable to those powerful vested interests mentioned above.

On our arrival in Nepal in 1978, we discovered wide-spread interest in basic needs in Kathmandu, but only as part of rural development, the latter itself an adjunct to a national policy of increasing agricultural output. Under such circumstances, an investigation, using a methodology appropriate to investigate an independent "basic needs strategy", seemed both necessary and timely.

From our investigation we concluded that a basic needs strategy must aim to provide the deprived and poor with the means to escape from their deprivation and poverty, not as a result of their identification as a "target" for assistance from above, but through their own involvement in the process of development and most crucially through their greater control over production, and thus over the conditions under which deprivation and poverty are generated and reproduced. Given this finding there must be some question regarding the practical capacity of the Nepalese State to implement such a strategy, bearing in mind its character, described in this and the first Chapter.

One of the greatest dangers is that, under those circumstances where the central and crucial elements of the basic needs strategy are perceived as threatening and/or difficult to implement for political as well as for practical reasons, they will be ignored or incorporated merely within a chastened and hence ineffective version of the basic needs strategy. In the "tamed" version of the basic needs strategy, the problem is identified as being simply about consumption (poverty), and not at all about control over and effectiveness of production; consequently the strategy to *eliminate poverty* becomes one which concentrates on the distribution of goods and facilities for consumption by "the poor" (e.g. schools, hospitals, subsidised housing, food programmes and, ultimately, famine relief). When distribution through the market (in the form of "trickle-down") visibly fails to fulfill basic needs, then the State is optimistically invoked as an institution capable of intervening "on behalf of the people" to provide them with essential goods and facilities. Such an approach overlooks the fact that the poor "consumers" (the target of the tamed basic needs strategy) are in fact the direct *producers* whose labour generates the wealth of the country, but who have little control over the means of production or of distribution. It also overlooks the existence of social class relations and the fact that these relations are expressed in the structure of the State apparatus itself - which inevitably represents the contradictions and conflicts within the political economy of which it is a part.

Thus our conception of basic needs, initially derived from the current debates in academic literature, was further developed by our findings in the field. These findings, however acquired their full significance only in the light of a firm understanding of the nature of the Nepalese State, the situation of conflict between the deprived and poor and those in power over them, and the fact that while their basic needs are now much talked about in the capital, there is very little evidence of provision. Our previous four years work in Nepal produced the understanding which we had at the outset of our revisit, and enabled us to get quickly into the field with a methodology which served our growing appreciation of the need to follow through the implications of a basic needs strategy determinedly in the Nepalese context. The fieldwork sought to uncover the actual position of the most deprived, as they saw it, and to use a methodology which would most faithfully represent their view.

Some Case Studies

In previous sections in this Chapter the general context of the lives of the deprived and poor has been described, and various categories of this (large) group analysed in a preliminary fashion. In this section we present some detailed case studies from the 77 households which we re-interviewed in 1978 as examples of particular households attempting to cope in different ways with the bleak predicament already described. They are transcripts from our field notebooks and preserve in some cases the direct speech of the respondents. The cast studies were chosen as broadly representative of a range of circumstances and responses to them (in the sense of not being chosen with a particular bias in mind - for example extreme poverty).

(a) Household in a Terai Village, 70kms East of Butwal

(The village in which this household was situated is a roadside village at the edge of the terai jungle at the juncture between hill and plain. Soil fertility is still high, and there is a large paddy and wheat surplus with a relatively large acreage under sugar-cane.) Interviewee (30 years old), wife (25), and 1 son (6), 1 daughter (8), with 1 daughter who died two years ago (aged 6 days), and old mother-in-law. Wife obviously dominant in household, since the husband is very oppressed, under-nourished, over-worked and probably chronically affected by parasites (he complained of weakness and a swollen stomach). He was ill two months last year while employed as a permanent labourer (*haruwa*) by a local landlord. He had no money, so received no treatment, and the landlord gave him reduced rations (about 60kg of unhusked paddy a month). It took three or four days pleading on the part of the wife to beg it from the landlord. Wife also occasionally finds daily paid labour (*mazdoor*), but only 8-12 days a year, and the old mother about a week's work (rate of pay about Rs.4/- per day). Thus income consists of about Rs.100/- from the *mazdoor* work of the two women and 900kg of unhusked paddy, 9 litres of cooking oil, 4kg of dried pulse, and 5kg of salt, paid by the landlord per year to the husband, for which the husband works 365 days a year and is "on call" from the landlord from 6a.m. to 6p.m. (and sometimes longer during times of peak labour demand). He also sells about 170kg of paddy to realise his cash needs. Two years ago he sold a goat for Rs.70/-.

The household consumes per year in terms of commodities which must be purchased by cash: meat and distilled liquor (for two festivals) Rs.24/-, spices 50/-, salt 100/-, cooking oil 80/-, kerosene 100/-, clothing 80/-.

Other assets include a straw house (four metres by three, costing about Rs.20/-), two goats and one chicken, and three cooking pots.

Their usual diet is rice and salt. No member of the family had drunk milk in the past year. Very occasionally the landlord gives him vegetables and pulse. The family eat together (like in most low caste and poorer households), and hence consume relatively equally. No in debt, and no real difficulty in feeding his family except a week or so in July. He could not beg rice at that time and all went hungry.

"I do not like *haruwa*, the landlord abuses me ... I don't like it." He worked as a weekly paid labourer (Rs.42/- per week) for four years on a highway construction project until there were no more opportunities. Prefers to work as a daily labourer but takes the yearly contract as a *haruwa* labourer because of the security it provides.

He left his *haruwa* contract one year in an attempt to register some land in the jungle (which exists in a broad belt at the foot of the hills in the *terai*). About fifty from the village decided to cultivate some land at the edge of the jungle. Each household according to its ability to clear the land, cleared a plot and planted crops. This continued for three years until "a government man" (most likely the Forest Guards) deliberately drove cattle across the fields, and burnt a hut that had been built on one of the plots. He and a crowd of others went to the local District Headquarters in Parasi to see the Chief District Officer, but were told to "come tomorrow with your applications to register the land". No one know how to read or write, and they got the help from a literate *Tharu* who filled in some applications. "Again we went, but they put some of us in prison". He avoided arrest and does not know the details.

In the last five years, the household has got poorer. No land, but more family consumption and the old mother-in-law cannot work much any more. His father and grandfather has no land. Neither he, his wife nor children have received any education.

(b) Household in a Terai Village 20kms South-West of Tribeni

Interviewee (husband, 35), two wives, 1 boy (first wife's, 12), 2 girls (6 and 5). No experience of child/infant mortality. Main income sources:

a) Own land, (0.33ha). Government has not stopped him cultivating land, but he has been unable to register it. Has tried to do so with the help of *pradhan panch*, and has filed application, three or four years ago. No reply. Produces 50kg of unhusked rice, a little pulse (very poor, sandy soil). Four-five hours away at edge of jungle.

b) Share-cropped land, (0.08ha), producing 150kg unhusked rice and sugar cane (not cut yet), from *Tharu* small landlord. Had it for six years.

c) Two oxen, which he hires out (with himself); payment 4.87kg unhusked rice plus Rs.5/-. The first wife collects the grass for the oxen.

d) Daily wage labour (*mazdoor*), for two months continuously. Ploughing for wheat (four months), building houses and contract labour for weeding sugar cane and digging (with a small band of other labourers). Second wife does *mazdoor* too, but less often and only weeding and transplanting paddy. Pay for women variable - 3.66kg unhusked rice per day for harvesting for 15 days, equal pay men and women. Very insistent on the superiority of *mazdoor* over *haruwa* for the labourer and also, for certain jobs, contract labouring. For house building, and some *mazdoor* he waits in his house until the employer calls him. For contract and other *mazdoor*, these are arranged with employers while on the job. No competition with migrants over jobs or land.

e) Selling goats - sold four two years ago for Rs.120/- each to finance consumption. Has now, two oxen, one calf (cow died last year, and *three* goats this year ... "Will buy more when I can save, maybe next year or the year after").

Had permanent labouring job (*haruwa*) two years ago but left it for *mazdoor* work on the Gandaki irrigation project. Worked there for two years, good pay (Rs.5/- - 10/- per day, or 30 - 50/- per week). After project finished, many labourers who had left haruwa for it never returned, having learnt that *mazdoor* gives better pay, more spare time and flexibility. But "we didn't discuss this, we made up our own minds".

Annual household expenditures: cloth Rs.150/-, kerosene 80/-, spices 100/-, pulse 30/-salt 100kg. p.a. (including feed for stock), barber 6/-; plus purchased rice (but gradually, so doesn't know how much).

Father and mother died when he was very small. Had 1ha. of land when he died. "Perhaps the land was sold". Has elder brother, now in a nearby village. Father died in smallpox epidemic. Elder brother had to beg at the time of father's death (*Tharus* were very generous). Lost land because rich purchasers of land bribed the factor of the local Rana estate to sell the land that had been held and worked (though not registered) by Chamar, poor *Tharu*, and other deprived groups. Not clear whether the severe de-population and dislocation caused by the epidemic was the *only* reason for the land being sold, or whether it coincided with land reform - probably not, since it happened about 30 years ago under the last days of the Rana regime, where land reform was unheard of.

Son goes to school (12 years old, but only in 1st class - "my son is stupid but I want education for him so as he can get a government job). Girls do not go, but I will definitely send them (for literacy only"). He and wives never went to school.

He himself is on the Ward Committee of the village *panchayat*. Ate rice and curry today, at home. Buys milk occasionally (one time per month, for guests and festivals). All eat together at the same time. But is often quite hungry, especially in July/August. Takes loan from landlord and repays in labour. Usually small loan of rice. Not in debt now. Has not had serious illness in family in last three years.

(c) Three Households in a Roadside Terai Village

Ram Bahadur Gurung has no land but used to have a small hut which he had built himself beside the road between Butwal and Bhairahawa in Anandaban *panchayat.* Some years ago however the local authorities widened the road and demolished his home. He received no compensation and has much to say about the arbitrary interventions of the State in the lives of the poor. An ex-soldier in the Indian army, he receives a pension of 960 Indian rupees a year, which supplements his income from *mazdoori* labouring of between Rs.600 and 700. He now "rents" a ramshackle building in the compound of a wealthy Newar farmer and merchant, who has first call on his labour and pays five rupees a day. "Four days' work for him pays the rent", he joked; and was at pains to explain the difference between this arrangement, with a nominal rent of Rs.20 a month and first call on labour, and the permanent labour relationship called *haruwa.* He distinguished between permanent haruwa, temporary or seasonal *haruwa*, and *mazdoori*, the three forms of employment differing according to their length of "contract" and degree of dependency on the employer. He argued that there were now fewer *haruwa* than before, partly because more landowners were sharecropping and partly because the labourers were no longer prepared to accept the oppression of the permanent labour relationship. On the other hand, he was himself becoming increasingly concerned, as a *mazdoori* labourer employed on a daily basis for the most part and a man of 50, about his future ability to maintain his large family. Four daughters by his first wife (who died some eight years before, apparently of diarrhoea and vomiting, at the age of 38), two small boys and two small girls by his second wife, and his present wife herself all depended on his income; for his eldest son by the first wife was now married and had a family of his own to support by *mazdoori* labour. His expenses frequently outstrip his income and when we talked to him he was in debt to the tune of Rs.400/-. and seriously concerned about his ability to reply.

(d) Hem Nath Brahmin

Also of Anandaban *panchayat* in the *terai*, was found to be seriously ill and barely able to speak. He insisted, however, on explaining how he had come to live as a virtual beggar on the front porch of a low-caste ("untouchable") but relatively wealthy Sunar's (Goldsmith) house, and his barely audible mutterings were interpreted for us by his ten year old daughter. An elderly man in an extremely emaciated condition, he depended largely on the generosity of the Goldsmith whose porch he occupied and who came from the same hill village originally, and on making up horoscopes and performing *puja* ceremonies. He and his little daughter lived on an annual income of no more than Rs.350/- and on gifts.

Originating from a hill village in Gulmi district where he owned a small parcel of land, he was obliged in 1971 to emigrate to maintain his wife and three children. He sold the land and came to the terai to buy land there. He was unable to find an adequate plot with the small sum at his disposal and set up a tea shop in the meanwhile to keep the family alive. The tiny business survived for around three years, but he was obliged to extend credit to maintain a clientele and when he fell sick with cholera four years ago the accumulated debts of between Rs.700/- and 800/- could not be recouped and the hospital charges led to his financial collapse. His wife returned to the hills with their youngest son of five to live with his wife's brother, and his other son of thirteen had to be sent to stay with his mother's brother in India. The only member of his family remaining with him is his ten year old daughter. "I have no land and no place in my village now; I am sick and can barely work. I may not see my family again".

The degradation for a high caste Brahmin involved in living on the porch of an untouchable was for him, as a priest, more hurtful than the extreme poverty and even the probability of not seeing his family or home again, and yet he said of the Goldsmith, "though he is untouchable, he helps me; he is a good man".

(e) Suk Lal Parsa, of Bhairahawa

In his early thirties and lives with his wife and mother in a hovel on the outskirts of the town. His wife and he have no children, which is a matter of considerable regret, but also a financial relief in view of his extreme poverty. His father had been a farmer, without land but renting it from others, but on his death some ten years before there had been debts to repay and Suk Lal has been obliged to work as a labourer in order to maintain the remaining, all female, members of the family. His only sister died about two years ago, with some intestinal disease, and his aged grandmother only six months later. His mother is too weak to work and even to do anything around the home, and his wife looks after her much of the time, trying to obtain short-term casual employment when possible (which is rare). At the time we talked to him he had been unemployed for over a month and was desperate; his wife was unwell at the time and complained of constant headaches, and he feared she might need medical attention. The household was surviving on a tiny amount of savings and on a loan of foodstuffs worth about Rs.40/- from a shopkeeper who had employed him previously. No interest was to be paid on this loan, nor was there a repayment date - "it is just help, and without such help we would not be able to go on". Suk Lal was bitter about the lack of assistance from any government department and the absence of any form of social security in Nepal. He knew of the existence of a few local"welfare associations" but pointed out that casual workers were virtually unable to organise such institutions themselves owing to the transient nature of their employment. The interview was brief for Suk Lal was unable to continue, saying finally: "I do not wish to speak to you about these things, for my situation is so miserable and I am so desperate that I cannot go on talking of them. It si not words that can change my life, but a change in my country, in Nepal."

(f) Household in Hill Village 20 mins. Walk from Kusma

(This village has a relatively large amount of irrigated paddy fields and is one of the most strongly surplus hill villages in the region. However the land holdings are highly concentrated, and agricultural labourers in this village are enmeshed in onerous relations of debt and dependency with landlords).

Interviewee (40), wife, 3 sons (20, married, 6, 1«), 1 daughter (9), 3 died (2 sons in infancy, 1 daughter aged 3). Has 0.05ha of unirrigable (*pakho*) land. Also lays claim to some *sukhumbasi* land (land, usually in or at the edge of the jungle which is cleared and cultivated "illegally", and not registered at the Land Tax Office). "But the rich men took it away. It is only used now for cows (rich men's cows). Our forefathers cultivated the land, and three years ago we also planted crops there. The *pradhan panch* (village headman) and his brother told us that we could not cultivate. We were very angry, and about 20 of us went to the Chief District Officer (CDO) to complain. The CDO said that we could graze cows only there. Now we are forbidden by the *pradhan panch* to do that sometimes."

Production: Maize 200kg, millet 130kg, some dried beans (about 10kg), a few other beans, no vegetables. Has one she-buffalo, two calves, one ox (shares to make up pair). Eats meat three times a year at festivals, no fish, eggs. Milk to children (0.20 litres a day). But ate yesterday, rice, pulse and vegetables because festival day. Had to purchase a further 100kg maize. (Estimated that one man eats 130kg maize per year). Consumption of cash items: salt RS.20/- (8 *pathi*); no oil, no spices, 5 litres kerosene (has to work sewing machine at night); cloth Rs.100/-, (about Rs.300/- per year in total).

Has own sewing machine. Had to get loan to buy it (Rs.360/-) and paid back nearly all (doesn't know the exact amount paid, but about Rs.450/-).

Earns cash by:

a) Portering merchandise along the trail between Syangja and Naudanda. 15/- per day at current rates, 1-2 times a month for six months. Very hard work and can only manage it once or twice a month. Also has to wait 1-2 days in order to get work.

b) Two months *"tekha"* (like short-term *haruwa* where a short-term contract for a month or two is undertaken between labourer and employer, the latter having call on the former's time 12 hours a day) for son and himself. 6a.m. - 6p.m., 70-100kg grain (usually maize). Maximum 120kg. Bargaining required over amount of grain paid.

c) A little sewing work - piece work. About 50-70kg maize.

His father had "a lot" of land but had to sell all but 0.15ha to pay off debts (land purchased by one of the present large landowners of the village). Interviewee had three brothers, so each brother only inherited 0.05ha each. Also the father had a bista, a customary arrangement whereby households in the village pay a fixed amount of grain to the artisan household (tailors, blacksmiths and shoemakers) once or twice a year in return for services on demand. As indicated elsewhere in this report, this custom is declining in many areas with a concomitant loss of income for "occupational" castes.

Member of ward committee in village, but "we have no power to do anything". Neither he nor his wife went to school, although the six-year old son does. Never had any hospital treatment although wife had severe bronchitis for five months. Eventually purchased medicine (cost 50/-) for her in Kusma bazaar.

Very conscious of exploitation, and the relations between landlord/creditor/employer and landless/endebted/employee. Has definitely got poorer in last ten years.

(g) Household in a Hill Village, Four Hours Walk from Kusma

(This village is one of the poorer villages in the area, located on a north facing slope, at high altitudes, and is extremely prone to hail storms which often destroy the maize and potato crops (two of the three staple crops) during May/ June. Very little irrigated land and many ex-army pensioners).

Interviewee (45), wife, one son (18 - left home, in India), two daughters (16 and 11), two sons died in last five years (aged 1, 1½). No money for medical treatment of children. Has land producing 170kg maize, 200kg millet, 6kg soybean. Has five chickens (one egg a week, the chickens are not for eating). Works as daily labourer (*mazdoor*) two months, every day for Rs.5-6/- per day or 3.4kg millet or maize - choice. Usually chooses latter because needs to eat immediately. Wants more work but very little in the village. Even advantaged peasants have insufficient food grains in some years (usually due to hail), and do not consequently employ agricultural labourers. Has to buy about 500/- worth of grain and household needs p.a. (50kg rice, 5.6 litres kerosene, 7 litres cooking oil and cloth costing about 200/-). Took loan of Rs.700/ - two years ago (having paid off a Rs.200/- loan six years ago).

Did some carpentry (but only Rs.6/- a day and seldom available). Son went to Indian army, doesn't send money, hasn't heard from him yet. Both daughters at school.

At time of interview has not food in house and no money (700/- loan all gone). Tomorrow? "I'll work for tomorrow". Always successful in getting food today for work tomorrow. When he was sick for three months (fever in August), his family (son and wife) found mazdoor work. Wife now does some mazdoor work (half as much as when he was sick). Gets paid the same as the men - in maize planting season and getting grass and firewood for richer households during the winter months. The family ate rice today (but only because others had repaired his house - free, but he was obliged to feed them rice). House was leaking and he called upon his neighbours to re-thatch and repair roof timbers (four men worked for about 4-6 hours). They eat meat four times a year, sometimes a little raki (distilled liquor) three times a year, and are often hungry. Children do not drink milk, nor eat fish, eggs, meat and very little pulse (household consumes few times per month, plus a little soybean). "We have all been ill, many times", usually coughs and fever but never any money for treatment (hospital is four hours walk away). "Sometimes we beg a little food when we are all ill and cannot work".

The forest has declined and firewood is a real problem now, requiring an eight hour expedition to gather enough wood for three days in winter. Also declining yields in the fields because no manure from the forest.

Not noticeably poorer during the last ten years, but much poorer since father's time since interviewee had one brother and inherited only half his father's land.

(h) Household in a Hill Village, Six Hours Walk from Syangja

(The village is a minor trading centre on a saddle between two hills, its relative prosperity is reflected in a locally constructed infrastructure which includes piped drinking water, middle schools, a health post and forest wardens; however, iron mining, which ceased about 50 years ago, has largely exhausted local forest.)

Household interviewed consisted of a woman, aged around 35, and three children, a daughter aged 14 and two sons aged 8 and 2 months. The woman comes from an ethnic group, the Newar, usually engaged in shop-keeping. Her parents owned a general groceries shop in the village and some unirrigated land. Her marriage was arranged when she was 17 with her cousin. Seven years after her marriage her husband went to work in the Calcutta police force and she moved back into her parent's house. After three years service in the police her husband resigned and came back complaining of illness. Soon after getting back the husband made a serious attempt to murder his wife. The domestic situation deteriorated over the following years to the extent that she went back to live with her parents. On the death of her parents her brother took over their house and business and she went to work in a roadside settlement about a day's walk away as a casual labourer in three tea-shops. Her husband followed her there and again beat her. After being arrested he was released after a couple of days because his behaviour was good; after a second beating, a second arrest, a second release the woman decided to return to the village with him as he demanded.

On her return the beatings continued and fellow villagers intervened in attempts to physically restrain him during violent periods and formally constrain him by signing a promise of good behaviour (to which the husband appended "signed under duress"!). Both methods failed particularly due to the fact that he caused nobody else trouble and on the contrary had a reputation as "a good worker" because he "does not stop for rest" (according to several villagers). The woman now lives with her children on a neighbour's charity. Her husband lives in the ruin of their former house, has sold the household's land and retains the gold his wife was given at marriage. With no money for books her eldest son has stopped going to school and the children's future will be as labourers unless the mother's brothers succeed in finding her a new husband.

(i) Household in a Hill Village Four Hours Walk from Syangja

(This village is in a wide valley bottom with good rice growing potential and a large annual fair. Recently farmers have started growing two crops of rice a year; the infrastructure of the village includes a health post and high school but productive resources are all privately controlled by powerful families including those of forests and water).

The household reported here consisted of a man (aged about 40), his wife and three young children aged between 1 and 7. The man's first wife and daughter both died about ten years ago and his son by that marriage (aged about 17) has left home and lives locally by portering, contributing nothing to the family budget. The household is landless and lives in a former cow-shed, rent free but with no security of tenure. Although the family name of the household is conventionally associated with being a blacksmith in the caste system, no members of the family have been blacksmiths for the last two generations. The household has benefited from the changes in agriculture in a number of ways but still remains desperately poor. The benefits include being able to give up portering "before it killed me" (an "economic" load is around

40kg). It is perhaps no coincidence that local porters have recently been able to collectively obtain an increase in rates of pay. He has also given up a ploughing bista, a form of tied labour relationship, and is successfully avoiding repaying loans/pay advances from former employers by refusing to work for them. However in terms of significant gains he has failed to secure land for sharecropping (because owners "like employing, not sharing") and has had no rise in wages from his increased productivity as a labourer, in fact, he considers wages have fallen as prices of purchased consumption goods have risen relatively (one employer argued that "real wages have not fallen" because the amount of food-grain made as payment has not diminished). The arrangements for recruiting have also not changed with a pool of about a dozen employers who "call" the labourer a few days before the work is to be done. By this method the labourer gets around one hundred and fifty days of work a year.

As mentioned above the family live in a cow-shed, one-roomed, stone built with a leaf thatch roof which needs annual renewal (straw thatch would cost Rs.100 so the household begs leaves from forest "owners"). Daily food consumption is supplemented be begging and varies from one to three kgs of flour a day for the family with salt.

It was reported that milk and fish were never consumed, meat was consumed only at the two major festivals, and even vegetables only a few times a month. Cloth was begged and since giving up portering the household "virtually do not handle cash". Sickness and death were a prominent part of experience as the first wife and daughter of the head of household had died, the present wife had needed recent treatment for "general debilitation" and the head of household himself had been unable to work for three days in the previous week because of illness. As a gesture of defiance in face of local oppressors the household (along with other poor households) had refused to work as "voluntary" labour on the local high school project which would have cost scarce energy and wages with no benefit to the household.

(j) Household Near a Motorable Road in the Hills

(This village is in a river valley with a large number of irrigable fields on which an early crop of rice has recently been tried. Some benefits from roadside location have been some bulking-up and breaking-down functions and a little commerce, about ten shops).

The household described here had six members. A man and wife in their late thirties with four children, a daughter aged 14 and three sons aged, 12, 8 and 2. Another daughter had died at the age of 3 of an untreated illness.The household had sold a house in a nearby off-road village to repay father's debts and moved to a well-made two-room house rented for Rs.30 a month. But this move had not resulted in the severing of former relationships. Nine households provided income from a mixture of tailoring, ploughing and general agricultural labouring on the basis of an annual payment augmented by donations for a machine and small loans for medical treatment and funeral expenses on favourable terms (i.e. 10 per cent p.a. compared with 3-5 per cent per *month* on credit from shop-keepers). In addition the head of household hopes to benefit from patronage by gaining access to land on a share-cropper basis. Seen in this light, an existing sharing arrangement of two buffalo and a pig (tended primarily by the daughter) is regarded as a hopeful sign by the head of household and, indeed, he regarded himself as fortunate compared with a brother who had migrated to the inner *terai* because the brother lacks the security of prosperous patrons. However the household only derives about half its income from these "patrons" the rest being earned from over 50 other customers for tailoring, labouring and portering work, plus music-making at marriages which is a conventional activity for those with the caste-name Damai.

This casual income, which depends strongly on the favourable location, does not protect the household from poverty. The household does eat about 2kg of food-grain a day with pulse but meat is eaten only a few times a year and milk and vegetables only when donated by employing households. Rent absorbs almost half the cash handled by the household and it seems probable that the arrival of a few more "tailoring" households in the area, an increase in availability of ready-made clothing or a rise in house rents would leave this household very exposed economically. The children have not attended school and the health of the wife is poor. The household has arrived at a "survival position" resting on continued dependence but the calculations involved are sensitive to many of the current trends in the wider economy.

(k) Household on the Fringe of Pokhara

(Pokhara is the regional headquarters with a population of around 25,000, most of whom still look to agriculture for a considerable portion of their income).

This household consists of a widow and three children (two daughters aged 22 and 16 and a son aged 18). An elder sone is a minor government employee in the terai but sends very little back in remittances. The son was interviewed during a break from ploughing which he does in the school holidays to help pay for his school expenses. Neither daughter has had any schooling and at present provide the bulk of the family income, the mother being too sick for work after losing an eye in an accident last year. The daughters have work for much of the year, finding up to six months agricultural labouring, and collecting firewood for at least two months. This now requires 12 hours work a day with the cutting of the forest. The household possesses little land (half their land was recently compulsorily purchased for a women's training centre) providing a small fraction of the family's food-grain requirements (about 50 days) and needing about a week's labouring. The son sees his future in "escaping from being a farmer" probably in government service. Being of Chhetri caste this is a possibility for him although this appears to be at the cost of the daughters' opportunities; even the spending of the proceeds from the land sale must await the decision of the elder brother working in the *terai*.

Consumption levels for the household are relatively high with over two kg of food-grain being eaten per day with pulse, vegetables and milk from the two remaining cows (three other cattle died of untreated disease last year). However the household has debts due to two misfortunes, the mother's medical treatment and the loss of crops due to hail last year. The total loans received by the household amount to about Rs.1,000 on which interest is paid to "relatives" in the village. The integration of this household with others is also indicated by the existence of reciprocal labour relations with about 40 other households (it is these households which also provide paid agricultural labouring). In addition to education for the sons and support from relatively prosperous "relatives", the location of the household close to the wider labour market of Pokhara has produced benefits in rising wages although how far this represents a rise in real wages is very questionable.

From these case studies, the diversity of individual situations does not mask the underlying element which we consider must be analysed in a study of basic needs requirements, namely: relations between the deprived and those in power over them locally and nationally. The possibility of implementing a "basic needs" strategy in Nepal must be considered in this context, just as it is in this context that the poor themselves struggle against deprivation.

NOTES

13. Nepal as a whole has one of the highest densities of cattle per head in the world.

3
THE STRUGGLE AGAINST DEPRIVATION

The Setting of Struggle for "Basic Needs"

In the context of a research programme concerned centrally with the problem of fulfilling "basic needs", it is important to focus attention on the *struggles of the most deprived and desperate*; consequently, we shall present our fieldwork from the perspective of these sections of the local population. It is thus that we can best examine the idea that deprivation and poverty are the products of a *complex structure of relationships* which involve deprived households with others in more privileged and powerful positions within the wider political economy. As we have tried to outline in the previous Chapter, the struggle of the deprived is not simply against "natural" circumstances, but against the social constraints which derive from this complex structure of social relationships. Thus general tendencies and trends identifiable must be seen as the product of the actions of people struggling to improve their material and social condition.

Given the desperately low levels of consumption of the households interviewed it might seem appropriate to view their actions solely from the analytical position of "survival strategies". Whilst this concept is useful it does have some shortcomings, primarily because the term "survival" suggests a too limited set of constraints and there is a danger of dismissing the radical element in the struggles by the deprived which seek to change the present political and socio-economic framework in which they are enmeshed. Also by limiting the analysis to survival strategies alone it becomes more difficult to see elements in such struggles which lead, however slowly, to the reorganisation of production to increase output and reduce exploitation. Lastly the term "strategy" itself suggests too certain a view of a particular future, whilst we would tend to emphasize the flexibility and uncertainty which out interviewees displayed when faced with new situations.

Thus in summarising the results from all our seventy-seven interviews we discuss the struggle against deprivation in terms of three types of action taken by the deprived and poor. The first is concerned with the immediate search for food and security, frequently manipulating patron-client relationships and their contradictions in order to provide the most elementary condition of existence. The second is concerned with actions directed towards securing private ownership of the means of production (i.e. achieving the status of an independent peasant), almost invariably against great odds and rarely successful. The third group includes those actions which seek to move beyond the relations implied by caste and patron-client, and to confront (either consciously or unconsciously) the ideology of individual liberty linked to private property as the only image of a good and just society.

The Search for Food and Security

The vast majority of households interviewed lived under conditions of great material deprivation, no matter whether viewed from the perspective of nutrition, clothing or shelter. For example we recorded cases of totally incapacitating adult ill health at the time of interview in 15 our of 77 households and a high incidence of child mortality (60 deaths reported in 45 households asked this question explicitly). Most households possessed no stock of food-grain and/or cash to purchase food-grain for the next meal. Our interviewing period was not the most difficult of the year (which frequently occurs in June/July before the maize crop for hill households) but we feel confident in concluding that frequent statements of days in this period without food for any member of these households were true and reveal the seriousness of their difficulties. In such circumstances the activity of the household is dominated by the search for food on days when no work is available. It was in this context of a daily yet chronic shortage of the basic necessities of life with a fundamental insecurity that our interviewed households acted.

In cases of temporary and exceptional misfortune (which can occur quite often in extremely poor households) gifts are sometimes forthcoming from other households in a fundamentally similar socio-economic situation but which find themselves temporarily relatively advantaged. The limits of such redistribution are soon reached and in a situation of widespread extreme poverty the deprived must use relationships with richer households in a mode of "institutionalised" begging of wide socio-economic significance. The vast majority of poor households had relations with at least five and in some cases up to 20 potential or actual employers who could be visited in the hope of begging a little food-grain for the next meal. Almost invariably the poor household performed some labour service during the year for each richer household, e.g. tailoring, repairing tools, house construction, agricultural and other labouring, portering (especially for shopkeepers). Thus considerable ambiguity existed around the nature of reciprocation expected. Was the food a gift, or an advance on wages, or a credit sale with or without interest? The manipulation of this ambiguity was often perceived as an arena of struggle by both parties. From the point of view of the poor, it was important to separate the gifts of food-grain from any future obligation. Two tactics exist to achieve this, firstly using rivalries between patrons and, secondly, spacing demands on any particular patron.

Where the agricultural system in a village produced a critical shortage of labour even for a short period, this allowed labourers to maintain incomes at a bare subsistence by "efficient" begging, where seeking a wage rise would meet unified resistance from employers. Begging plays its role in socially reproducing a labour force in conditions of servility and dependence at a bare subsistence level. In this sense the form in which income is received is as important as the amount of income. Outside such direct "patron/client" relationships two major alternatives exist for a poor household to gain sufficient food to subsist. The first is food from the jungle in the form of roots and berries. No households reported significant food gained from this source; even those households which were most chronically malnourished reported low availability of such food. In the absence of supplies of such "free" food the only choice left for rural households is to diminish the demand for food by reducing the number of individuals. Children given into service of richer households are at least ensured of some food every day and a poor woman who moves to a new richer husband suffers little loss in status compared with the possible gain in material security. This breakdown of families, excluding migration of young men, was found in thirteen households. Among poorer households no significant dowries were paid and so martial breakdown was rarely complicated by division of assets apart from tiny amounts of jewellery. The high incidence of single parent families is thus probably not a cause but a result of poverty. As a solidarity group, even the family thus shows some signs of fragility in the face of socially crippling poverty. In some cases we did observe great mutual support between men and women and parents and children, but such support was by no means so sure as to make the family the obvious unit of any basic needs strategy. In the struggle for survival no relationship can be treated as sacrosanct and unquestionable.

In circumstances of such desperate material deprivation, which incidentally include many small cultivators as well as the landless, it is to be expected that accumulations of food-grain in the hands of individuals or the State will occasionally provoke a violent response. In the area we studied, the most striking example of an attempt at violent redistribution sparked off by such accumulation was reported in 1969. The introduction of a State compulsory savings scheme in the form of food-grains during the second half of the 1960s produced considerable pressure on many small farmers and resulted in great hardship for a significant number whose savings, except in a good year, could be made only out of current consumption. During 1967 and 1968 the Nepalese press reported that ward committees were not keeping adequate records of savings collected, that committee members and other locally influential people were misappropriating the savings, and that resistance to payment was growing. Finally, in April 1969, protest against the compulsory savings scheme turned to violence. The trouble reportedly began in Tulihawa, the administrative centre of Kapilvastu district, when a crowd of village women surrounded and attacked officials attempting to collect compulsory savings. Violence quickly spread across Kapilvastu district and into Rupendehi district. Looting and police firings occurred in a thirty village area over a three-week period. During this period, at least twenty-three persons lost their lives, hundreds were wounded and many others arrested. Compulsory savings depots and private homes were looted and burned.

The Nepalese newspaper, "Gorkhapatra" summarised the official view of these disturbances on 15th April, 1969: "Complete tranquillity now prevails in the villages of Rupandehi and Kapilvastu District where compulsory savings had been looted ... Part of compulsory savings in kind looted in some of the villages of Rupendehi District has been recovered. During the disturbance savings were looted in about 50 villages of Rupendehi District and at the Suani Village of Kapilvastu ... According to local administration, the disturbances in the two districts were instigated by both political elements and dacoits. Concerned official circles believe that few Nepalis living in exile in India, some Indians who have been trying to settle down in Nepal and some Indian dacoits had a hand in these disturbances."

In our view such an explanation cannot account for such widespread disturbances.

In a situation where local welfare provision is tied to the very conditions which reproduce poverty and central authorities take no responsibility for feeding the undernourished, there is an incentive for welfare organisation among the poor themselves where circumstances are favourable. Such circumstances occur in towns where larger concentrations of population exist. For example, the attempt to form an independent rickshaw association in the southern town of Bhairahawa in 1974-75 was initially founded on the notion of providing a fund from which those suffering road accidents and other misfortunes experienced as a result of their occupation could draw in times of need. For the motor transport sector, a Transport Workers' association was founded in 1974 and is still active in 1978 with over 600 members suffering accidents during their work. Families of men who die during their work in transport receive financial and other assistance, as do individuals maimed or crippled during their work. The Transport Workers' association also operates a small clinic with two visiting doctors "for the poor" and provides donations for medical provision, such as the provision of an ambulance for the Butwal hospital and the equipment of an eye hospital at Manigram. Rotating credit associations, such as those among muleteers in the north, frequently include conditions which allow them to operate in part as welfare associations insofar as credit may be taken at times of crisis for consumption purposes as well as for investment.

While these associations (welfare associations and credit associations) have clear and limited objectives, they have a potential as the basis for more general forms of collective action to improve the bargaining power of the relatively deprived and disadvantaged. In the early days of the industrial revolution in England, for example, there were no bodies that could properly be called "Trades Unions"; nevertheless, there were in many towns firmly-established "trade clubs", containing workmen in particular occupations. These ran sickness and burial funds for their members, but gradually they tended to join together over a wider area and to become more like trades unions defending and promoting specific interests - those of the relatively weak. Thus the organisation by the deprived to gain minimal material security can overflow into wider spheres to tackle the origins of poverty.

The formation of such organisations and their stress upon independent mutual support among the deprived constitutes an active denial of the economic basis of the caste system with its emphasis upon a hierarchical pattern of distribution. This, in turn, raises the question of actively denying the legitimacy of discrimination on caste grounds. In towns, relationships based on caste related occupations are weakest and thus conditions are best for an association explicitly attacking that aspect of basic needs deprivation associated with social prejudice. Such an association of "untouchables", (the Dalit Jana), is concerned to promote and defend the situation of the "low caste" and so-called "untouchables" in Nepal. While some of the leaders and activists in this national association (which has several branches within the West Central region) are relatively rich, coming from professional or business families, the vast majority of the rank and file are not only socially and religiously discriminated against, they are also generally among the poorest and most disadvantaged people in Nepalese society.

Unlike the other "cultural" associations in Nepal, the Dalit Jana Association has far wider economic and political objectives in addition to its caste basis. It is concerned with the transformation of Nepalese society, through education and collective action where necessary, to eliminate the bases of economic, social and religious discrimination against the "low caste" peoples and to provide the means whereby these particularly disadvantaged sectors of Nepalese society may be able to improve their economic status whatever their occupation. Founded over forty years ago, what is now the Dalit Jana Vikash Parishad has provided during that period an organisational framework within which collective action could be undertaken, both nationally and locally, to improve and defend the living and working conditions of "low caste" people. It alone acts to mediate between individuals of "low caste" and employers, officials and other more powerful interests when situations of conflict occur, invoking the existing laws and decrees against discrimination and for the welfare and safeguarding of the interests of the disadvantaged and deprived and ensuring their application.

The efforts of the State apparatus itself to initiate "self-help" schemes in villages and small towns could be expected both to be directed towards the very poor and deprived in terms of the construction of facilities as well as of remuneration for work done. "Community projects" initiated by the village *panchayats* very frequently expose a frustrated paternalism among *panchayat* leaders interviewed who were caught between a failure to extract resources from the generally richer and "high caste" households and resentment of their unpaid labour extracted, often under duress, from the poorer, lower caste households. The resolution of this dilemma in the villages visited was found to be the undertaking of local projects whose likely benefits to the deprived were zero, using unpaid labour from the poor. In one case a group of the poor refused to labour without pay on a high-school project. This attempt to assert themselves was successful, but in most others the threat of prosecution for unpaid fines produced grudging compliance. Thus, at the village level the vestiges of the caste system play a role in legitimating the obligations of the "low caste" and the rights of the "high caste", reproducing in the development project the division of labour where manual work is the lot of the "low caste". Furthermore, the choice of project frequently reflects the needs of the advantaged rather than the deprived. Drinking water projects are a major exception - and even here the siting of taps and design of the water system is frequently controlled by caste considerations where avoiding ritual pollution of the higher castes becomes an important factor.

As a conclusion to this section it is clear that the implementation of a "basic needs" programme even in the field of elementary welfare provision cannot rely upon altruism from the advantaged. Rather guarantees of food and security can only occur with the active participation of the deprived themselves as a part of a much wider set of changes attacking social prejudice itself in all its forms. For those born poor and of "low caste", the struggle to achieve the former is intimately involved with attempts to escape the latter.

The Search for Ownership of the Means of Production

The search for access to productive resources was found to be always difficult and sometimes dangerous - difficult because discrimination operated to informally debar many households (e.g. where the heads of households were women or "low caste"), and dangerous when the search involved direct clashes with the State apparatus in its coercive and oppressive role e.g. in preserving the forest against sukhumbasi (landless squatters). In a situation of resources declining both absolutely and per capita, a search for productive resources is a zero sum game. However, for most individual households no better alternative could be envisaged, and much of the activity we observed in our fieldwork was directed towards this end.

For landless households the physical reminder of land-ownership is often close at hand in the form of particular fields cultivated by this, or the previous generation. The loss of this land was often associated with perceived fraud by other households personally known to the members of the now landless household, rather than fragmentation on inheritance or "natural" disaster. Discrimination on caste (perhaps due to loss of caste in an inter-caste marriage) or sexual grounds played a role in making it difficult for the losing household to gain adequate compensation within the immediate community. Occasionally action took the form of an appeal for justice outside the village, but this was almost always precluded by lack of financial resources, leaving the household dependent on limited support from households linked by kin or patronage relationships. Our fieldwork found twenty-one examples of lost productive resources which will illustrate these dynamics in practice.

Four households had experienced loss attributable to natural calamity, since our previous survey in 1974-75 -

"natural" in the sense that death of livestock (two cases) or landslides (two cases) were not attributed by the household to specific human agents. Of course, poor households were more vulnerable to loss of such resources since they had vulnerable fields or limited fodder availability but in these four cases some economic recovery had been made with assistance from fellow villagers. All the remaining seventeen households could identify, with varying degrees of specificity, the social cause of their loss. This is not to dismiss the grave ecological crisis presently threatening Nepal, but to say it is only one determinant of the process of deprivation. The trauma of loss of life and land experienced in"natural" disasters attracts world publicity, while the continuing and far more pervasive "social" disasters remain unreported. Basic needs investigations may help redress this balance.

In Nepal, the low level of health service provision combined with hazardous working conditions leaves large numbers of children orphaned in each successive generation. The rights over land of such children are conventionally vested in an adult male (usually a senior relative) until the child reaches maturity. During the child's minority, therefore, such rights are vulnerable to loss. The cases we met included two where the cruelty of the "guardians" resulted in the children leaving the home area and becoming vagrants, whilst in two other cases, despite the continued presence of the "owners" in the area, the land was appropriated on the basis that the child's father had forfeited the rights as repayment for unrecorded debts. A fifth case is an example of the active role caste discrimination can play in the redistribution of real resources. In this case, inter-caste marriage provided the rationale for loss of inheritance rights, leaving one line of a family without property.

A process of social deprivation can also be seen operating in the present for twelve households. In three cases, women were faced with bringing up children in situations where "inadequate" husbands had transferred land to unscrupulous relatives and/or neighbours. In two cases, the land of the household was perpetually in danger of moving from ownership under mortgage into total loss. Claimed debt from the previous generation and the costs of fighting a court case to register rights over land formed the basis of this vulnerability. The role of the State in widening the area of vulnerability and turning that vulnerability into actual loss of control over land was evident in the remaining seven cases. Two households had land compulsorily removed by the State for "development" projects. One household received no compensation for the loss of land as a result of a road-widening project - but the second had been paid close to a market (albeit a very limited market) value. Both however had lost control over the means of production and became vulnerable to further loss. The remaining five had engaged themselves in a common struggle to register rights over land which they had customarily cultivated. Here the State had not only failed to recognise such rights, but acted to imprison members of the households for debts to their employers who were rivals for the control of the disputed land. The identification of local power with central power was a shared experience for all the households who had "lost" land through social action; appeals to formal administrative or judicial authority invariably had been dismissed or, where counter claims by powerful local interests were made, over-ruled with costs being borne by the weak whose position was thus further eroded.

Those households with no previous title to land adopted four types of strategy to gain control over resources. Two involved accommodation with local power structures and two by-passing local power and seeking legitimation of claim directly from the central authorities. These strategies in practice tend to either overlap or escalate into each other but the classification is useful to provide a framework for discussion. This is illustrated in Table 11.

The majority of households interviewed still possessed strong individual ties with patrons, despite the tendency to move towards more impersonal market relations. In all cases these households were struggling to loosen these ties towards independent control over some area of production. Labourers sought share-cropping and animal-sharing arrangements in the hope of securing a toe-hold in the climb towards ownership rights as a reward for loyalty. Artisans improved their productive potential through new equipment and/or alternative location with loans from richer clients in order not so much to provide a better service to the existing clientele but in the hope of extending their activity. It is tempting to conclude from the evidence of our interviews that, in general, the tension between actual dependence and hoped-for independence is doomed to be resolved in the direction of the former. However, it is sometimes in the interests of local power-holders to give limited rights to their dependents. The threat of land reform imposing a maximum land-holding may split some local power interests from simple identity with central power, encouraging at least nominal distribution towards trusted dependents. Also animal health risk-avoidance encourages dispersal of control over livestock on a basis of shares over subsequent off-spring. In several locations visited virtually all the breeding of oxen was undertaken on this basis by labouring and artisan households. Thus the hope of independence through this route for a limited number of households is not totally illusory.

Table 11

A TYPOLOGY OF STRATEGIES ADOPTED TO GAIN CONTROL OVER PRODUCTIVE RESOURCES

	Type of Activity	
Primary Direction of Activity	*Individual*	*Collective*
Local Power Holders	Extension of existing patron/cllient relations	Use of "communal" resources, e.g. forests and rivers
Representatives of Central Power	Purchase and registration of Property rights	Settlement on uncultivated land and struggle for security of tenure arrangements

Closely associated with the ability to maintain livestock are customary rights at a local level over forest and pasture land. Whilst such rights are almost invariably exercised individually, they are seen as communal in essence so that attacks upon them are met collectively. Thus attempted restrictions on access to forests, pasture and rivers were, in two villages visited, forced to take account of the common protests of the landless if open conflict was to be avoided. However, in these struggles the State representatives were attempting to intervene to "protect" the resource base, thus reducing the ability of the weaker sections of society to maintain this limited independence. Whilst we would not argue against the principle of safeguarding the rural ecology by restrictions on individual exploitation of natural resources, the prevention of such destruction does involve present sacrifices, and it is the nature and distribution of these sacrifices which concern us here. Insofar as the "ecological problem" is isolated from its general context and treated as a technical problem of selecting types of treesor crops and restricting access for a gestation period, then the distribution of sacrifices will at best reflect other inequalities and, in practice, will deepen inequality. Thus caught between physical loss of common resources by over-use and political loss through restriction on access this is a struggle that the deprived cannot win, especially as they possess no mechanism for guaranteeing any share in the future benefits which present sacrifices may produce.

Thus struggle at the local level in support of customary rights is finally frustrated by official State policy which emphasizes the rights of private property and consequently land sale and purchase (even to the extent of encouraging privately owned forests). Only those households with considerable cash can gain control over productive resources by acting in the realm of legal contract and thus by-passing any objecting local power holders. Two households interviewed had earned sufficient outside Nepal to purchase land on return of the head of household, and two others had regained control over land which had been lost through debt. Also five households managed to gain sufficient finance by astute trading to emerge in a slightly stronger position with respect to an overall balance of assets and liabilities. This was balanced by an equal number of households who had lost control over resources through the initial sale of land in a desperate move to improve immediate consumption. From this evidence it is difficult to make the case that the development of market relations (outside the labour market) is likely to improve fundamentally the basic needs position of many households, rather it involves a redistribution of productive assets with little prospect of increasing production.

The legitimacy of the State as the representative of the people and an instrument for curtailing oppression of local power structures has not been accepted by most interviewed households. Where the interests of local power holders and of the State were not seen as identical, the interviewees perceived the government as an independent source of domination, and not as a defence of the deprived against local oppression. This was particularly explicit in struggles over the control of uncultivated land in the terai, where the malaria eradication programme has opened up a frontier for settlement in the last twenty years. Severe restriction on settlement by the Forestry Department has produced a major struggle directly and visibly between the deprived and the government. Two examples are briefly discussed here, one from our own recent fieldwork, and the other as documented in the Nepalese press.

The first example refers to current attempts revealed in ten interviews conducted in March to register previous "waste land" cleared and cultivated on the edge of the forest in the *terai*. In one *panchayat* investigated some thirty household heads of various castes prepared applications for individual registration of land plots of less than 1 *bigha* (2/3 ha). These were taken jointly by the heads of the households to the Chief District Officer. The response of the CDO to the joint application was simply to evade the issue; in contrast, the response of the Forestry Department to the cultivation by these households of marginal land at the edge of the forest was to wipe out the standing crops and the temporary houses which the cultivators had built on or near the land in dispute. The cultivators repeated their visit to the CDO on several subsequent occasions to press for the registration of "their" land - but to no avail.

The second example refers to events reported in the Nepalese press in 1966. In September 1966 a crowd estimated at around 4,000 collected around the administrative headquarters of Nawal Parasi district in Parasi village and, according to official reports, "rioted and threatened the lives of government officials". The demonstration was claimed by local people we interviewed to have been due to threatened non-registration by State officials of the land ownership rights of large numbers of cultivators. The response to this large-scale collective action by the police was immediate. According to official reports, nine persons were killed and another twelve wounded in the shooting that followed. The legitimation for such action was provided by the Palace Secretariat of the Royal Palace in an official report: "a huge mob headed towards the police headquarters on 7th September and the number of police personnel was insignificant in proportion to it. It is thus evident that the firing was justified". The publicly released version of the report contained no explanation of the riots and unofficial investigations were discouraged. The Government-sponsored Peasants Organisation expressed the view, however, that the disturbance was at least partly the result of "citizenship problems" (involving small cultivators and tenants of Indian origin) arising from the abolition of the Ukhada land-tenure system, especially in Nawal Parasi and Rupendehi districts. The Nepal Times observed that "the official report which was released immediately after the firing disclosed that the mob responsible for the unhappy incident was incited by certain undesirable elements. But the enquiry commission report does not make any reference to such elements. The report does not give any convincing facts as to how thousands of people could be incited by a handful of undesirable elements". The Naya Samaj reported that "Our Bhairahawa correspondent has written that the kind of people who had organised the procession does not suggest that the procession was taken out to oppose the Land Reform Programme and the Ukhada Land Tenure System".

In some contrast to the sporadic, if spectacular, events associated with the struggle to increase control over production in the countryside stand the forms of struggle in the towns. Here organisation is more formal and in its collective aspect goes beyond an immediate objective of securing individual control but involves a longer-term expression of a shared interest among the relatively disadvantaged, even if here also they are often defeated. For example, attempts were made during 1974-75 by some of the rickshaw pullers in Bhairahawa to form an association, one of whose objectives was to control the rents demanded from pullers by those renting out rickshaws. In 1976, in Butwal, led by four experienced rickshaw pullers, the rickshaw pullers called a one-day strike whose objective was to maintain the rent of rickshaws at Rs.6/- a day. They visited the town *panchayat* and obtained verbal support from officials; they then attempted to form a syndicate to control rents and charges to passengers. In response to this action by the rickshaw pullers, the owners (the rentiers) also visited the town *panchayat* and made clear their unwillingness to accept the terms of the pullers; they refused to hire rickshaws to the leaders of the strike at any price and the movement collapsed. The rentiers then successfully put up rents to Rs.7/- per day.

Small producers and artisans in the urban areas, such as tailors, cobblers and others, frequently face considerable difficulties in raising sufficient cash to purchase necessary equipment or to maintain their businesses. In this region of Nepal, a specific form of rotating credit association (*dhikuri*), originally operated in the mountain areas of the far north and historically associated with a particular ethnic group (the Thakalis), is much used by businessmen generally, including artisans. Some of these associations consist entirely of very small artisans, petty commodity producers and retailers, who by co-operating in such an association are able to raise funds that individually they might not be able to do without entering into an arrangement with a money-lender. Several examples of such credit associations involving tailors, cobblers, small goldsmiths, petty retailers of various kinds, and others were identified. through these credit associations small producers are often able to obtain funds to purchase equipment (such as sewing machines, lasts and other items) for their businesses. In cases where smaller and larger businessmen combine to form a credit association, the smaller tend to take the funds earliest; consequently, they often use the association to establish a business, paying back into the fund over a longer period of time after having taken a loan from it. Financial advantages certainly derive from taking the fund later - a fact of which both larger and small businessmen are very aware - since the rate of interest effectively obtained by those who wait until last is considerably lower than that which they could obtain as private moneylenders. The credit association thus provided a certain welfare function and credit on relatively advantageous terms for the small businessman.

Thus the struggle for control of productive resources at the household level is not totally doomed. But in the rural areas, where the identification of the government with local power interests is most complete, then the disadvantaged find exclusion is backed by officials, the police, and the judiciary (see case studies). Virtually all the households interviewed had experienced oppression of this type in their struggles and, in the absence of any independent rights to representation, they regarded the government as an important active agent in their deprivation. Thus they dismissed land reform and other such legislation as at best, window-dressing and, more sinisterly, as an attempt to legally establish inequality by formalising individual property rights in favour of the prosperous in cases where ambiguity over control previously existed.

The Search for Better Labouring Conditions

A crucial feature of the households selected for interview was heavy involvement in labouring for others. However within this category there were found a number of types of relationship. Our fieldwork was centrally concerned to investigate how labourers struggled to change these relationships which were central to their deprivation. These struggles concerned higher wages, shorter hours of work, control over type of task performed, and rates of activity-these were all stated as important by interviewees. Thus labouring was not seen only as a means to a consumption end, but to some degree as an end in itself, a source of satisfaction when performed at a pace dictated by the labourer.

Those involved in a *haruwa*, or "permanent labouring" arrangement were least able to act independently, as they were required to attend from sunrise to sunset at the employer's house every day of the year's contract. But movement between employers on completion of contract was common and acknowledged as an important means of gaining better working conditions, despite the general uniformity of the level of payment. Often the extent of advance payment rather than the total payment was a crucial factor and underlines the debilitating effect the lack of grain reserves on the part of the labourer has upon their ability to press demands for better pay more militantly. Nevertheless the desired move from a previous employer could frequently be made. Opportunities for this arose with large-scale development projects, e.g. highway construction and irrigation canals, but the rewards from such projects are structured against saving and at the end of such projects labourers were frequently forced back reluctantly into haruwa relationships on exactly the same terms as previously.

Significant amounts of non-agricultural labouring were rarely available locally and so the search for wages outside the restrictions of local agriculture frequently took people away from the household. Types of migration differed widely, ranging from a few weeks construction labouring in a town a few days' walk away, to decades in an Indian city. Occasionally considerable fortunes are made in activities undertaken during migration, but more often only bare subsistence is obtained. Most households had members with recent experience of life in Indian cities and thus had no illusions about conditions for the unskilled without contacts. The temporary nature of such migration indicated that migration, except possibly as a recruit to a foreign army (only possible for some), is regarded as poorly as "permanent labouring" as an activity. A regional pattern of deprived young men being permanent labourers in the terai and temporary migrants to India in the hills suggests that this equivalence holds.

Invariably the most preferred situation was that of a local daily paid labourer with regular employment. This was not due to higher incomes, since though the equivalent daily wage for a permanent labourer was lower, there was no guarantee of employment on a daily paid basis for the whole of the year. Reasons for preference included the possibility of choosing between employers, choosing to take days off, shorter working hours, and choice of tasks. The preference for local employment allowing the labourer to play a role in the general life of the household was indicated by considerable differences in wage rates between villages only a few hours' travel apart, but this also reflected the recruitment system in that labourers waited in their houses to be called by an employer. Only in the peak agricultural seasons were there sufficient potential employers for the labourer to exercise some choice. Under exceptionally favourable circumstances of an expanding local economy and low dependency ratio, some households were able to totally subsist on local daily-paid labouring. Such households regarded their position as relatively fortunate compared with neighbours tied to particular employers.

Whilst generally, the position of labour is weak, the existence of occasional labour shortages in time and space is recognised by both employers and employees. In such circumstances we found groups of labourers bargaining with potential employers or arguing with existing employers about rates of pay, and tasks to be done. For instance, in one *panchayat* in the hills a group of labourers collectively negotiated a higher rate of pay for portering, and in another *panchayat* in the *terai* teams of men were formed which undertook work on a piece-work basis sharing wages equally. This had started in the sphere of sugar-cane harvesting but was spreading into other agricultural activities also. Rather than waiting as individuals to be called by an employer and allowing the employer then effectively to create a workforce, individual labourers were forming work-teams or work-groups of their own, and then negotiating with employers on this basis. Where local employment was limited, such work teams or work gangs moved on a wider basis round the region. On occasion these gangs will travel considerable distances to find employment, usually outside agriculture. For example, gangs were identified in the town of Pokhara which had been formed in villages in other districts, travelled together to the town and sought employment, usually in construction or road-mending as a gang.

Collective action on an extended basis to improve working conditions or to raise wages generally is rare in the rural areas; no organisation exists which defends and promotes the interests of agricultural labourers or other workers in the rural areas. In the urban areas it is also rare, despite the existence until 1976 of an official Government-sponsored Workers Organisation. Given the small size of most enterprises in the urban areas, and the high turnover of labour, collective action is limited. In a few cases, however, notably in the larger establishment, there are signs of increasing preparedness to resort to collective action to improve working conditions and wage rates. In March 1978 workers at four major enterprises in Butwal in the *terai* were planning to hold a joint meeting to demand minimum wage levels and daily allowance - while at the largest factory in the region (the Mahendra Sugar Mill) several strikes with similar objectives had occurred over the past few years after other forms of negotiation had failed.

During the fifteen or so years of its existence, the official Workers' Class Organisation was not able to build up a significant degree of popular support and participation, but it did provide recognised channels and vehicles for collective action by groups of workers. Despite limited achievements they managed in some cases to establish the existence of a relatively autonomous sphere of action beside the hierarchy of *panchayat* representation. In the West Central Region the Workers' Association provided some degree of support for workers in their workplace, at least in establishments employing more than ten persons, and had some small impact in encouraging workers to act collectively in defence of their interests (as in the case of the 1976 strike at the Mahendra Sugar Mill). The other "class organisation" were (in 1974-75 and 1978 at least) either non-existent or relatively ineffective.

Towards a Framework Linking Action and Policy

In the previous Chapter we described the specific experiences of a number of households and in this Chapter we have discussed the actions which all the interviewed households undertook in attempts to achieve their basic needs. In this section households and actions are recombined so as to relate the characteristics of the household to the type of action they take. What any particular household can do depends on factors which seen together we call the "access profile" of that household. Access has a number of dimensions including *physical access* - proximity to other households thus permitting a certain level of the division of labour; ecological conditions including proneness to erosion and availability of forest; and availability of markets through a modern transport network. Equally important for the households we interviewed were questions of *economic access*; e.g. a bus fare, *social access*, e.g. belonging to a group permitted to handle food for others, and *political access*, e.g. someone to plead a case with local officials. Certain general processes are occurring which alter access profiles for the deprived. These processes link the actions of households interviewed with the national crisis that we described in the first Chapter.

Most villages in Nepal are becoming increasingly incorporated into a single national Nepalese economy and are integrated with each other to some extent through a growing market economy. Both the "internal" system of exchange (encouraged by complementarities within localities caused by the different production possibilities associated with physiographic variations of terrain) and an "external" market (through which mass-manufactured goods from India now substitute in consumption for the home-grown and manufactured items e.g. cotton yarn and cloth, shoes, kitchenware, waterpots, agricultural implements, soap, lamp oil, etc.) developed partially as a result of changes in relationships within the villages. The growing demand for cash elicited a variety of responses from those households who still had some measure of control over the means of production (i.e. small peasants and artisans). One was emigration in search of land and/or wage work, and another, for those who stayed, petty commodity production tended to increase. Large numbers of households started to produce small amounts of a wide variety of commodities using household labour for the market to meet cash deficiencies.

A new kind of access and a redefinition of value both resulted from this development. The household was forced to match its physical access to a market to its existing control over means of production, both "public" (e.g. forests and rivers) and "private" (land and labour). Within the broad regional framework of opportunities for producing for the market, the individual household has to choose increasingly in what ways and to what extent it will enter the market. This calculation is determined by the household's access to productive resources, now regarded as sources of values in exchange, exacerbating the plight of those discriminated against (i.e. women and "low castes") in access to such resources.

Rather different are the responses of the completely landless who either are permanent labourers (*haruwa*) or pursue daily wage labour (*mazdoori*). In those areas where extensive land grants were made by the ruling aristocracy over the last 150 years and have partially survived land reform, large production units continue to be controlled by one household and worked by "permanent" (and frequently this amounts to bonded) labour. Labourers often live on the farm itself, are paid in kind and have a personal non-market relationship with the employer, secured through debt or sharecropping arrangement. The increased necessity for cash purchases and other pressures deriving from the division of holdings, increasing family size and in some cases declining soil fertility has tended to be reflected by increased efforts on the part of employers to make a more intensive use of employees' time, and to reduce informal "perks", bonuses, quasi-gifts to permanent labourers. However, because many landowners are not forced to enter the market, they continue to dispose of surpluses locally and to relatives, and are reluctant to invest in farm equipment or other inputs.

The labourers to possess a minimal level of material security in basic consumption, although access to social provision like education and the law is limited. There is some control over productive resources held on a sharecropping basis, not only land but also animals. But minimal security focuses the problem of oppression as a denial of a "basic need". The ties to the landlord/employer constrain the ability of the disadvantaged to participate fully in all spheres of life. Politically, culturally and in the work situation the "permanent labourers" are stifled in expressing themselves compared with poor peasants and even wage labourers who are their neighbours. The tendency away from such arrangements thus tends to be welcomed by the labourers themselves whenever the reduced security of wage labour can be tolerated.

Households which have shortfalls in the production of food-grains and do not have access to non-agricultural income nor the necessary resources for adequate petty commodity production need to work as casual labourers whenever possible. Because some part of the cost of reproduction of the labourer is borne by production in the wage labourer's household, the wages paid by employing farmers are close to the point which is only sufficient to feed the labourer whilst working. Since productivity rises very considerably following any "capitalistic" investment in new inputs, and real wage levels have been constant for at least thirty years, the surpluses derived from these labourers' migrations has increased greatly. The transient nature of the labour force, its commitment to domestic production for at least part of the year in many cases, and its diverse ethnic background, tends to inhibit effective organisation by labourers. Only in situations where a wage labour force is kept together for longer periods than the agricultural busy season, can the conflict of interests between employer and employee produce organised action to improve working conditions and, then, the officials have generally been willing to intervene on behalf of the employers.

These broad processes of change form a framework in which households' access profiles are being continuously modified and thus sets of possible actions changed. For the purpose of this discussion the current actions available for the interviewed households can be divided into four sub-sets:

a) *Perpetuated dependency:* actions in this sub-set include begging and "loans" from fellow-villagers including employers, income from the communal resources of the village and selling productive assets including land. All these actions are vulnerable to the general directions of change described above in which market relationships are replacing paternalistic considerations, and in which the labour market is becoming increasingly saturated, not only because of an increase in the supply of labour (landless and sub-marginal peasant) but because of a decline in the demand for local labour.

b) *Peasant aspirations:* such actions include purchasing assets or seeking sharecropping arrangements and private attempts to register land in the name of the household. Whilst such actions go beyond the simple "survival strategies" of (a), they again are vulnerable to the erosion of particularistic relationships which give some households a relative advantage, and to a relentless reduction in the amount of unclaimed land left.

c) *Conventional alternatives:* migration of all types and the general search for non-agricultural income have been a feature of life for the deprived for over 150 years; more recently attempts to benefit from the expansion of the State apparatus (especially elementary schooling for children) and approaches to officials for advice and assistance have also become significant. None of these activities are likely to become more attractive in the future as general competition for work in manufacturing and the bureaucracy becomes fiercer with more people seeking wage employment.

Table 12

A HYPOTHETICAL EXAMPLE OF A DYNAMIC FRAMEWORK FOR CLASSIFYING HOUSEHOLD ACTIONS

Household	*Types of Action*											
	a	*b*	*c*	*d*	*a*	*b*	*c*	*d*	*a*	*b*	*c*	*d*
1	Yes	Yes	Yes	Yes	Yes	Yes	Yes	Yes	Yes	Yes	Yes	Yes
2	Yes	Yes	Yes	No	Yes	Yes	Yes	Yes	No	No	Yes	Yes
3	Yes	Yes	No	No	Yes	Yes	Yes	No	Yes	No	Yes	Yes
4	Yes	Yes	No	No	Yes	No	No	No	No	No	No	Yes
5	Yes	No	No	No	Yes	No	Yes	Yes	No	No	No	Yes
6	Yes	No	No	No	No	No	Yes	No	No	Yes	Yes	No
Trends in the wider economy	"Past" Overall access situation a>b>c>d				"Present" Overall access situation a=c>b=d				"Future" Overall access situation a=b<c<d			

Key :
a: "Perpetuated dependence"
b: "Peasant aspirations"
c: "Conventional alternatives"
d: "New departures"

Increased outside Income Opportunities (c) and decline of settlement "frontier" (b)

Increased in daily-paid paid labouring and relative decline in all other opportunities

d) *New departures:* certain types of action can be characterised as "new" in that they are directed towards changing the conditions on which labour is employed and/or involve organisation among the deprived independently of patrons and government agencies. These departures are frequently actions taken unilaterally without consultation or combination with others and without a conscious political purpose. However, in a few cases (such as in land registration), collective action, albeit ephemeral, does result in a challenge to the State apparatus and the ideology which legitimises it.

Table 12 summarises this analytical framework in a tabular form. The dynamics are represented by three points in time ("past", "present" and "future") and the impact of processes of overall change upon access profiles of households and their consequent fields of action are shown. In the first period (an unspecified "past") deprived households act predominantly with particularistic relationships which give access to actions which offer survival as a client of local patrons (a) and the possibility of becoming more independent through gaining private control over productive resources (b). However, processes in the wider economy already described act to change the overall access situation against these actions and towards seeking other sources of income beyond previous patron-client relationship (c) and the emergence of clear wage-labour relationships and independent organisation among the deprived on behalf of the deprived (d). Of course this overall shift does not affect all households evenly since every household has a particular access profile at one point in time within the overall situation. For instance, household 4 is still able to act within an access profile emphasizing patronage and the search for control over productive resources. As we look towards the "future" the overall processes continue squeezing more households into new types of action with the possibility of mass organisation. Here patronage survives but has become less common.

Our hypothesis here is that our interviews approximate to a cross-sectional picture of households living in the "present" of our model. The results of the interviews are summarised in a format suitable for comparison with our model in Table 13. If we consider the overall situation initially by looking at the row labelled "total", almost one-third of the households interviewed were active in all four categories showing the manner in which many deprived households exercise initiative across the whole range of options. For those with more limited fields of action the category of "perpetuated dependence" is almost always exercised. Forms of patronage are still very important but closely followed by relationships which move beyond patronage albeit along lines which we treat as "conventional alternatives". Within this category almost half the households had recent experience of migration and a third had attempted to give children of the present generation some elementary schooling. Striking from the point of view of our hypothesis is that the majority of households had some experience of those actions we have called "new departures" - only a few less than those attempting to gain independent control of the means of production. The alternative hypothesis to our own that all landless, or near landless, households singlemindedly seek ownership of land regardless of situation is denied by this finding although if access profiles were modified in some hypothetical way in the direction of giving land to labourers then undoubtedly few would refuse!

A "regional" grouping of the households reveals some interesting variations on the overall pattern. In all the regions we found households active in all categories. Thus the "new departures" are not confined to particular types of location, but occur among all groups of households in rural and peri-urban areas in the hills and the rural *terai*.

An extended quantitative analysis of Table 13 is clearly not appropriate since cell sizes are small, and there existed a certain element of judgement on our part in assigning various actions of households to categories of action (a to d). However some interesting general indications of patterns of action emerge:

Table 13

INTERVIEW RESULTS GROUPED BY CATEGORIES OF ACTION WITHIN "REGIONS"

Number of households		*Number active in all categories*		*Number not active in category (*)*			
				a	*b*	*c*	*d*
"Rural" hills	29	10	(34)	0(0)	11(38)	1(3)	11(38)
"Peri-urban" hills	12	1	(8)	3(25)	4(33)	2(17)	8(67)
"Rural" *terai*	24	11	(46)	1(4)	6(25)	9 (38)	3(14)
"Peri-urban" *terai*	12	2	(17)	1(8)	6(50)	1(8)	8(67)
Total	77	24	(31)	5(7)	25(32)	13(19)	30(39)

(*) N.B. Some households inactive for more than one type of action

Number in brackets denote percentages in each cell of the total number of households in the appropriate row

Key: a: "Perpetuated dependence" c: "Conventional alternatives"

b: "Peasant aspiration" d: " New departures"

a) Households in peri-urban areas tend not to be involved in a large number of different actions as compared with rural households. Institutionalised begging and other actions which tend to reinforce dependency relations with employers appears to be uncommon. This may be explained by the limited basis for such relations, tied as they tend to be to notions of land-ownership, long-established employer-employee links between households of the same village, etc. This may be one of the reasons that the unfortunate households in peri-urban areas were among the most destitute and desperate, without even the opportunity of mortgaging their future labour time to borrow enough grain for today.

b) The differences between the rural hills and rural *terai* households are less marked than between rural and peri-urban households. However the households of the terai seem both to be involved in more new departures (usually a move from *haruwa* to *mazdoori* labour), and less the conventional alternatives such as out-migration. The hill households all involve themselves in institutional begging, and certainly their economic circumstances are generally even more dire than those in the *terai*.

c) Moving on now to comments on the columns in the matrix (where they have not already been made above), actions perpetuating dependence are the most common form overall, especially in the hills.

d) The move to control one's labour time by *mazdoori*, piece work or the formation of work gangs is still the least common, although the collective attempts to register land are widespread.

e) Overall, about a third of all households were involved in all four types of action. In the context of the previous discussion, a flexible, risk-averting general strategy, mixing individual and collective action (in the rare cases it was perceived as having some chance of success) was followed. Single actions by households were rare and vulnerable to failure.

So far the response on the part of the government to collective action has tended towards the openly coercive thus encouraging the escalation of violence by the deprived. In the name of liberty and the linked right to private property, the government has intervened on the side of employers whenever the power of employers over employees has been threatened. If our model of future changes in overall access patterns is correct then the government will be forced to meet such demands with violence on a wider and wider scale. The alternative is to create political conditions in which the interests of the deprived find legitimate independent expression. Conflict will still exist but perhaps not invariably end in violent confrontation. The dilemma of the ruling class is whether to continue to suppress directly or indirectly its opponents by systematically denying them "basic needs" or to risk an escalating series of demands which might result from making concessions which accept the political implications of a full "basic needs" programme.

In summary, the relevance of our framework to "basic needs" provision is straightforward. The deprived in Nepal have little reason to view the powerful at the local or central level with anything other than suspicion. Present trends point to an increased number of people who will have to find the means for existence outside systems of patronage. With the present crisis in production there are few unallocated resources, and given the structure of ownership there are no signs of existing resources being moved in directions of higher levels of productivity and employment. The irrelevance of the current rhetoric of popular participation through *panchayat* democracy, and of private property (where any, even academic or preliminary discussion of collective forms of ownership are usually suppressed), has become clear to the poor and deprived of Nepal. Distributional goals as implied by almost every recent policy or planning document in Nepal are in fact delusory, in the sense that powerful interests actively oppose the mass getting them, and illusory, in the sense that the productive base of the economy is too weak to allow everyone to achieve them.

4
BASIC NEEDS AND GOVERNMENT POLICY IN NEPAL

The Elements of a "Basic Needs" Strategy

The "basic needs" strategy (BNS) has its origins in the World Employment Programme launched by the ILO in 1969, a programme through which the ILO sought to pioneer a new employment-orientated approach to development. The findings of this programme are embodied in the ILO report *Employment Growth and Basic Needs* which was considered at the World Employment Conference in Geneva in June 1976. Since the Declaration of Principles and Programme of Action adopted by the World Employment Conference and endorsed by the United Nations General Assembly in 1976, the term "basic needs" has become widely used in debates on strategies for development both within the OECD Member countries and in the international development agencies.

BNS itself has acquired the status of a new conventional wisdom because of the obvious failure of the development policies in the past. The very poor were discovered to be more numerous than a decade ago, and BNS was conceived as a new response to this, particularly as a reaction against the discredited theories of "trickle-down" effects. The most important causes of the persistent reproduction of deprivation are: lack of access to the means of production (in terms of productive resources) as well as effective control over their use; yielding lack of access to the fruits of production; and a lack of participation in decisions (selection of needs, priorities and the means to achieve them). These elements are closely interrelated.

It has been argued that BNS should, in principle, be characterised by a careful assessment of the resources available, and of the means by which these resources are to be controlled and allocated (e.g. participation in the decisions which affect peoples' own lives, etc.). It should eschew the "income approach" to development as a method of identifying target groups and as a strategy which implies that basic needs can be fulfilled by a mere transfer of purchasing power to deprived groups. *Control* of *production* is thus at the centre of the "basic needs" approach to development, which implies a concern with the *political economy of deprivation*.

The Declaration of Principles Programme of Action specified that "strategies and national development plans and policies should include explicitly as a priority objective the promotion of employment and the satisfaction of the basic needs of each country's population" (Article 1). The "basic needs" strategy first of all aims at meeting the requirements of "the poor" for minimum consumption and essential services. In the words of the Declaration, "Basic Needs includes two elements: first, certain minimum requirements of a family for private consumption: adequate food, shelter and clothing, as well as certain household equipment and furniture. Second, they include drinking water, sanitation, public transport and cultural facilities" (Article 2). The "basic needs" strategy recognises the importance of democratic participation and accepts that "a basic-needs orientated policy implies the participation of the people in making the decisions which affect them through organisations of their own choice" (Article 3). It also emphasizes the notion of employment as a "basic need". "In all countries freely chosen employment enters into a basic needs policy both as a means and as an end. Employment yields output. It provides an income to the employed and gives an individual a feeling of self-respect, dignity and of being a worthy member of society" (Article 4).

"Basic needs" strategy, as outlined in the Declaration of Principles and Programme of Action, therefore, includes participation through organisations of their own choice by the mass of the people. At least one writer has recognised that a full acceptance of the terms of the basic needs strategy may have revolutionary implications (see Jean Majeres "Study on Popular Participation in Planning and Decision-Making for Basic Needs Fulfilment" for the ILO, 1977). If the term "revolutionary" is taken in its broadest sense, not to mean violent upheaval but a fundamental transformation possibly taking place over a considerable period of time, then we would accept that, in this sense, a "basic needs strategy" is inherently "revolutionary". It allows the deprived and the poor the means to escape from their deprivation and poverty, not through their identification as a "target" for assistance from above, but through their own involvement in the process of development, and, most crucially, through their greater *control* over *production*, and thus over the conditions under which deprivation and poverty are generated and reproduced.

This essential element of an effective BNS is inevitably in conflict with certain interests of the land-owning classes which are largely represented in the government and therefore can only be incorporated. Any reader of official policy statements cannot but be struck by the mention of "people-oriented development", concentration on the poor and landless, social justice, the aims of *panchayat* democracy, particularly in fostering participation by the people, and so on. Unfortunately, and not surprisingly, such sentiments remain rhetoric, and our fieldwork (as well as many other studies, both Nepalese and foreign) shows this.

In the tamed version of the "basic needs" strategy, "participation" becomes incorporated as a token, rather than as a central force behind the development strategy. In certain underdeveloped countries, participation and self-help *have* helped significantly to transform the economy and society *from below*, in the way that the "basic needs" strategy envisages; such countries have been relatively successful in providing "basic needs", but that success was inextricably associated with fundamental changes in the political economy as a whole. Where participation is reduced to a token involvement, the success of a "basic needs" strategy is thrown immediately into question.

Genuine involvement by the people "in making the decisions which affect them through organisations of their own choice" does not, of course, assure an immediate and dramatic transformation of the political economy and the consequent fulfilment of "basic needs", but it is, we would argue, a prerequisite - a necessary although not sufficient condition - for development. As the UNDP observed recently in their comments on a Strategy for Rural Development in Nepal,

> "There can be no panacea for rural development: the issues are inherently complex and related to the intricacies of agrarian society and of national socio-political setting... In order to successfully tackle the implementation of such strategy, a strong political determination is required." (UNDP 1978).

Basic Needs and New Thinking in Nepal

If one accepts the view of the UNDP expressed in the previous paragraph then it is absolutely crucial to be able to identify with some precision and some reliability from which social groups and categories *if at all*, the "political determination" required to implement an effective "basic needs" strategy is to come, and what alliance of interests are likely and possible to serve this end. Any suggestions or policy recommendations made must confront the problem of where, if at all, a "strong political determination" can come from - precisely because the need for such determination implies the existence of strong conservative entrenched interests which must be overcome.

It must be recognised from the outset, that any attempt to implement an effective "basic needs" strategy in Nepal (as almost certainly in other countries, albeit with differing characteristics) will inevitably confront opposition by vested interests, and that such interests are strongly represented within the government itself.

Given such an appreciation, it follows that the "basic needs" strategy must be specifically designed to meet the particular dynamic of Nepalese society in order to have the maximum likelihood of being adopted at all levels by all relevant groups. In order to bring about the fundamental transformation required, to err neither towards simple rhetoric nor towards over-ambitious programmes, requires a long-term programme of reform, based on those social groups and categories most likely, at any given point in time, to support the measures envisaged in a particular *stage* of the programme.

It follows from this that it is necessary to identify in advance the contemporary basis of a progressive alliance and also the probabilities of any future shift in alignments between social groups and categories to change the basis of progressive alliance in the future, in order to serve the needs of a "basic needs" strategy. It must be recognised that in the continuously changing configuration of the political economy, the elements of any progressive alliance will themselves be changing. Reliance on foreign aid, recognition of the crisis that we have described, the changing pattern of class relations within Nepal; all these interact and generate new possibilities for the implementation of a "basic needs" strategy.

We have argued together with other commentators on Nepal, that far-reaching structural change is required if the mass of people in Nepal are to be assured of their "basic needs" and that this implies the need for a strong political determination. It is encouraging to be able to join with the UNDP in their *Comments on a Strategy for Rural Development* in noting "the growing awareness of this necessity which implies far-reaching structural changes" (UNDP 1978).

There is evidence that some of the thinking behind the formulation of the "basic needs" strategy has begun to percolate into the writings and deliberations of some politicians, planners and other government officials in Kathmandu.

That elements of the new conventional wisdom of "basic needs" have begun to appear in official documents is not strange, given the importance of this approach in the international aid agencies and among many of the major aid giving countries, and the importance of foreign aid for Nepal. The existence in official documents of "basic needs" language must be seen not only as a product of irresolvable contradictions within the Nepalese political economy, but also as a contributory factor in encouraging real change.

In their discussion of "agricultural modernisation in Nepal" during a seminar on development in Nepal held in September 1976 in Kathmandu, two Nepalese researchers observed that

> "the process of development, in general ... (has) ... bypassed the people - the small farmers and the agricultural labourers. Thus the need for a change in the objectives of and approaches towards agricultural development is imperative. This, however, has only been realised recently by the people at the policy and planning levels" (Dhital & Yadhav 1976: 4-5).

Elsewhere Yadhav has written:

> "Till now the main lacuna in our objectives and strategy of agricultural development is an omission of the equity factor which must be deliberately imbedded in the programme itself rather than wait for the invisible hand' to take care of it" (Yadhave 1976: 14).

Similarly, the Times of India of 27th February, 1978 reported that:

> "A member of the national planning commission Mr Govind Prasad Lohani, has urged the upper and middle classes to identify themselves with problems faced by the masses who lived in poverty ... Mr Lothani, who made it clear that he was expressing his personal views, pointed out that the main impediment in utilising human resources for development were bigger rural interests' and supporters of capitalists within the government ... He said it was difficult to mobilise human resources in a big way in any multi-party system of government. Mass mobilisation for development was possible only with an organisation which was strong and reached out to every village."

While the above is, as stated, a personal view, it is encouraging that these sentiments were originally printed in the official Nepalese daily newspaper "Gorkhapatra" of 26th February, 1978, indicating that quite marked criticism of official policy and practice is being allowed a voice. This in itself is a partial admission by HMG of past mistakes, and by implication, of current policy measures being misdirected in some fields.

A critique of inadequacies in approaches adopted to date implies a recognition of the need to construct new integrated programmes. Thus in 1976 a Nepalese contributor to an international conference spoke in Bangkok of a need for integrated rural development arguing that:

> "Since there is little scope for bringing new land under cultivation in the Hills and Mountains and also that the Hill agriculture is already over-burdened it will practically be a difficult task to sustain even the existing people in the Hill agriculture at a present level of population growth, until and unless livestock programme is integrated into crop development programmes. *In the absence of such integrated programmes the poor would remain still poorer and our whole effort to provide a minimum level of food, clothes and shelter for these rural poor will be of little impact"* (Pant 1976: 3).

He also emphasized the need for action at the grass roots by the people themselves in local institutions.

> "After long experience of trial and error' in our development efforts, we have come to the conclusion that *raising the standard of the small farmers is possible only by development through institutions or group actions'. The basic idea behind this principle is that unless we mobilise and regenerate locally available capital and other resources in which human resource occupies an eminent place, a development programme no matter what it looks like cannot lead to a breakthrough in the rural areas"* (Pant 1976: 7-8).

Various attempts have been made to establish a co-operative movement and the rhetoric of Back to the Village was recently institutionalised:

"The principle of group action is well taken into account. All rural development efforts will be channelised through *'Sajha'*, a common co-operative venture, in each village panchayat. Human resources in this system will be mobilised by local institutions. The Back to the Village Campaign' at national level will supervise closely, through its district organisations, the development efforts of the local leaders and evaluate their performances in rural development." (Pant 1976: 7-8).

And certainly, the new emphasis upon District level development planning, and the earlier attempts by Back to the Village Campaign to nominate committed members to the panchayats from the deprived, represent welcome indications of a commitment in the direction of a redistribution of power. They do not, as yet however, go very far in either conception or implementation.

For example,

"the second part (of the planning process) will comprise those programmes so far implemented by district officers, ministries, departments and regional directorates but to be designated as district level projects by the government and those so far financed and managed by local panchayats." [Basic principles of the 6th Plan 1980-85 (Draft) p.1.]

With the right to decide being heavily qualified as follows:

"Panchayats in accordance with the *given objectives, policies, priorities and resources* of the 6th Plan will generally decide which projects will be undertaken by the Village and District Panchayats according to their requirements." (*Ibid* p.6, our emphasis).

However, this remaining limited autonomy at the village level does involve "basic needs" considerations:

> "The projects at the village or ward level should be productive, employment oriented and basic needs oriented and also ... must reflect the felt needs of the people." (Ibid p.9).

Unfortunately our fieldwork illustrates very clearly the type of project to be undertaken at the local level, namely those involving "voluntary" labour in so-called "public" works programmes to build schools, roads, and other facilities whose utility to the most disadvantaged and deprived (who provide the bulk of the unpaid labour) is questionable.

In a similar vein, official pronouncements on the role of co-operative movement (*Sajha*) emphasize its relevance to "basic needs" provision within a rural development framework. See Pant's remarks above. In the draft of the 6th Plan the role has grown:

> "Institutional development in the rural sector will also be sought by encouraging industries along co-operative lines (*Sajha*) and channelling agricultural credits and other inputs, marketing of agricultural products as well as other daily necessities through *Sajha*". (NPC, 1978, Chapter 2, p.11).

Nowhere in our fieldwork could we find any reason for this confidence and a recent report on the efficacy of co-operatives worldwide in third-world countries is equally sceptical (UNRISD, 1975).

It might be contended that Nepal is a candidate for an all-out growth strategy, aimed at stimulating agricultural production among "leading farmers", even if at a high social cost, and increasing differentiation. Such a strategy would assume that Nepal, lacking an indigenous capitalist revolution, could rapidly solve mounting food deficits by the introduction of a package of new technical inputs, aimed at generating a class of modern farmers from the rich peasantry and larger landlords. In our opinion, such a strategy has an extremely limited chance of achieving even its growth objective. If the use of new inputs is to take place on the scale necessary for significant growth, then crucial decisions concerning environmental management, the introduction of new crops, the replication of seeds suitable for local needs, the control of grazing and breeding of cattle, etc. must be taken on a collective basis. These collective decisions, if they are to be successful, must be implemented by the broad mass of people - not imposed by a few large farmers and backed up by a repressive state apparatus - otherwise the forest will continue to be raided by the poorest families, cattle will not be kept out of the paddy fields in winter to allow an extra crop of wheat to be planted; there will be little willing co-operation in small local public works programmes, or the establishment of local seed replication programmes, etc. Clearly Nepal needs rapid growth in agricultural production; our argument is that such growth *cannot* take place unless a "basic needs" strategy in the full sense is adopted.

There are clearly no simple policy recommendations which can be implemented to "solve" the problems of Nepal. Because of the nature of the constraints on the fulfilment of "basic needs" in the way we have defined them, individual projects and programmes emerging from a "basic needs" strategy can be expected at best to help generate other deeper changes needed to transform the political economy of Nepal and not, in themselves, to bring about the necessary transformation.

Existing Programmes: the Co-operative Movement

HMG in Nepal regards the co-operative movement as generally successful and an integral part of the development process in the rural areas. The 4th Plan was self-congratulatory but recognised deficiencies in co-operative formation and operation:

> "The co-operative system was introduced in the country during the first plan period. The increased number of societies indicates that there has been remarkable progress in this field ... These co-operatives were not merely developed by those people who accept the principles and the ideal(s) of the co-operative movement. They were formed by the Department of Co-operatives

with government grants. Therefore the existing co-operatives lack sufficient funds, members, knowledge and efficiency of management" (NPC, 1970: 82).

However, the 6th Plan seems to recognise no deficiencies in the co-operative network whatsoever. Co-operatives are seen as an ideal development institution. There now seems to be a firm belief at government level that the co-operative system is the most efficient and effective agent of change available to "basic needs" strategy in Nepal. It is firmly linked with the *panchayat* system, and so an apparently neat package of decision-making, technological improvement, distribution and marketing machinery results.

Although the Co-operative Department has existed since 1956, the renewed impetus of the movement aimed at the small farmer and the landless has only been identifiable in official policy since 1976. Implicit in the official view of co-operative institutions is the belief that they can only be beneficial to their members, and that benefits accruing to members are equitably spread. As, in HMG's view, prior inequalities among member households are irrelevant in determining the distribution of benefits within the co-operative, and furthermore HMG appears to believe that co-operative societies do benefit all their membership in most cases, the government only pursues the goal of inclusion of poorer households within the *Sajha* movement.

In general, though, the *Sajha* movement as presently constituted has only a very limited role to play in contributing to the provision of "basic needs" of the most vulnerable groups. Credit and agricultural inputs are seldom taken up by the smaller farmers. Though the co-operative acts as a supply depot for a variety of goods (e.g. kerosene) to the general public, the very poor cannot purchase small quantities of goods, since the co-operative sells without credit in standard units which exceed the cash limits of the poor family. The socio-economic heterogeneity of the membership and the directing influence of a central Ministry limit co-operatives in Nepal, much as they have in many other parts of the world, to contributing little to a "basic needs" strategy.

Insofar as co-operatives succeed the result is often the medium-term perpetuation of the peasantry, particularly the less advantaged sector, and in Nepal a fundamental doubt upon the long-term outcome must arise. First of all the section of the population at whom the schemes are directed itself is under serious threat - the small farmer of today is becoming the landless of tomorrow, when present trends within households are extrapolated. As landless, they are no longer within the purview of the co-operative movement. Secondly, under existing circumstances in Nepal, "co-operatives" linking households of unequal assets and associated unequal political power tend simply to exacerbate the loss of control over productive resources by the disadvantaged, for instance, in allocation of common land rights.

Indeed the major conclusion of a recent UNRISD Study of Co-operatives is that

> "rural co-operatives in developing areas today bring little benefit to the masses of poorer inhabitants of those areas and cannot generally be regarded as agents of change and development for such groups" (UNRISD, 1975).

The implications of such a negative conclusion must be seriously considered by policy makers and planners concerned with the condition of the most disadvantaged in rural Nepal.

The Small Farmers' Development Programme

In contrast to the *Sajha* movement, with its ideology of a self-evident common interest throughout Nepalese society, there have been recent attempts to deal with the problems of the disadvantaged through specific programmes. The major example of this shift in current official policy is the Small Farmers' Development Programme (SFDP), started in 1977 to encourage collective action by the poor in applying for credit, purchase of inputs, some agricultural operations and sale of outputs on a limited scale in a few localities. Such applications do not require security other than a joint statement of intent.

The Small Farmers' Development Programme attempts to tackle the production problem *directly* by providing virtually unsecured credit for investment by self-selected groups of very small farmers and landless. So far the Programme exists represented essentially by a pilot scheme in Nuwakot and Dhanushe Districts (not in our study area) to encourage action groups (smaller than the usual co-operative size) of between five and twenty households to identify projects which would assist in increasing productivity, incomes and employment opportunities. In Nuwakot 37 groups were formed of 665 individuals in total and in Dhanushe 32 groups of 312 individuals. The degree of ingenuity, enthusiasm and co-operation shown by the participants using tiny amounts of resources is reportedly great. Some doubts might be raised over this scheme's replication on a much wider scale; the initial costs of setting up the project are high in terms of the demand for committed and skilled assistance in dealing with physical and social barriers as they emerge. However, the cost of "administration" and management under a genuinely decentralised political structure, with executive power at the local level, is believed by advocates of the SFDP to fall rapidly as the participants themselves increasingly fulfilled the scheme's administrative requirements.

In spite of the many caveats (the cost of replication without effective decentralisation of political power and decision-making, and the self-defeating nature of encouraging, say, buffalo-rearing by the landless in terms of depleting critical resources), *this scheme directly seeks to fulfil "basic needs" by providing the opportunities for co-operative action, full participation, and increased productivity.* The movement towards recognition of a shared responsibility for ecological and social relationships by everyone involved will not be easy and will suffer many set-backs. Our fieldwork reveals a desire for that responsibility among the small farmers and landless but not if all the sacrifice is to be exacted from them with no compensation.

There are indications that an extension of the SFDP would be welcomed in some official quarters also. Kamla

Bhasin and Baljit Malik wrote in a recent article in the FAO paper "Bulletin 122" that:

> "Expansion of the project in many more areas of Nepal is what everyone is talking about now. In fact the ADB has already decided to extend it to fifteen more districts. Successful projects should indeed be multiplied, especially by SFDP as it is neither expensive nor does it require too many additional personnel or structures" (Bhasin and Malik, 1978: 20).

Similarly the outline of the 6th Plan explicitly mentions the Small Farmers' Development Programme not only in the context of extension to new locations but also in terms of extension of the principle involved:

> "The ongoing Small Farmers' Development Programme (SFDP) will be implemented in (a) more extensive and more effective manner and special programmes for improving employment and income opportunities of persons like rickshaw-pullers, cart drivers and others engaged in small business will likewise be launched in urban areas" (NPC, 1978: 10).

The above attitudes are to be welcomed, since the SFDP both concentrate on some of the poorest groups and will increase its scope to include those other people whose livelihood is increasingly bound up with deprivation among the mass of rural poor.

It was once considered, in some circles, that the ADB loans to small farmers would be a considerable risk, since no collateral is required. However, recent evidence suggests that in fact small farmers are a better credit risk than richer producers:

> "The repayment of loans is almost 100 per cent, thanks mainly to group responsibility and group pressure. With no default in repayment the small farmers have proved to be better borrowers than the rich farmers, whose default rates are quite high" (Bhasin and Malik, 1978: 17).

The present guidelines for the Agricultural Development Bank can be contrasted with those of the credit institutions operating under the earlier 4th Plan, for example, where:

> "Such institutional credit will be provided only on the condition that real tenants will be the owner-tillers and that the land for sale will be used as security against loans advanced to the tillers" (NPC, 1970: 54).

One of the fundamental elements of agrarian policy, which has been rarely questioned, is the individual ownership of land. But various schemes for "collective operatorship" with individual ownership have recently been put forward. One eminent Nepalese scholar, M.C.Regmi, has publicly suggested a scheme for *panchayat* land ownership, in which land is legally owned by the *panchayat*, but individuals use it by payment of rent to the *panchayat*, being free to sell such rights within certain restrictions. In this way surpluses accrue to the cultivator and the *panchayat* rather than to absentee landlords unlikely to re-invest locally. As more land came into the hands of the *panchayat* (since no land would revert to private ownership and control) it would start to dictate land use (grazing, arable, forest reserve, etc.). Common ownership combined with common operation of land in a country in which peasant proprietorship and landlordism both exist will only develop slowly and on a small scale initially.

While political decentralisation and increased representation of the majority (small farmers and landless labourers) might tend to improve the equity performance of co-operatives as distribution agents, the more fundamental consideration of collective control must be faced if the deprived and disadvantaged with little control at present over productive resources are to benefit significantly.

The Nepalese Crisis, Participation and the Disadvantaged

Whilst "self-help" programmes among the disadvantaged do have an important role to play in any "basic needs" strategy, the ecological situation in Nepal is such that it must be given specific attention in any development strategy. The 6th Plan recognises that a "basic needs" policy cannot concern itself merely with the provision of essential services to private individuals but must also provide for conservation measures for the common good, albeit only within the current private property ethic of the Nepalese State:

> "For the reason that the perpetual progress and the property of Nepal and the Nepalese depend upon conservation, development and the utilisation of natural resources, the 6th Plan will .... (aim at) ... safeguarding the continuous development process from all possible danger, maintaining a proper balance between nature, population and ecology by taking necessary measures against flood control for conserving and promoting forest and wildlife reserves and other natural and physical resources" (NPC, 1978: 8).

Through collective control over all land a number of important "policy" measures can be implemented much more effectively, and which contribute directly to the fulfilment of "basic needs", namely: reafforestation of areas under secondary forest and scrub, the planting of fodder trees on terrace backs, the growing of winter wheat (requiring a collective decision to exclude cattle from the winter grazing of arable land), local seed multiplication schemes, and minor irrigation schemes. Positive State intervention in these areas has so far generally proved ineffective, and in those cases where the State has been effective it has often been detrimental to the interests of the disadvantaged, (e.g. diminished access to common land for the poor without compensation and forced labour without reward and under the threat of fines and imprisonment).

Thus, in some of its aspects, the crisis itself is producing a growing awareness of the need for mass participation in implementing any development strategy, particularly at local project level. This awareness does not extend as yet to actively calling for participation in *determining* that strategy. Instead, the stress has been on participation in local decision-making as the only effective method of mobilising labour for implementing "boot-strap" rural development programmes. Participation was not seen, in the official view, as a political action. Hence the King stated, in 1970, that:

> "The manpower resources that are going to waste today could be mobilised, to the maximum extent possible, in a disciplined way for development work. In this task the co-operation of all classes, of panchayat and class organisations at different levels of the private sector and of the people in general is essential. It is therefore, my firm belief that full co-operation of every citizen in the country will be forthcoming in the sacred task of national development" (NPC, 1970: Preface).

By 1978, the language of "participation" and involvement" has become the common currency of many official pronouncements on development. For instance, the call for "broad-based and people-orientated development strategy enlisting people's participation and mobilising local resources and skill" (NPC, 1978: 6) and it is suggested that, "since rural development projects depend for their success on the co-operation of numerous small farmers, involvement of the beneficiaries is essential in both project planning and execution". (Ministry of Finance, January 1978). But structural changes in the political organisation of the decision-making process to improve access for the majority are not envisaged, for "In Nepal, participation of the people has been institutionalised in the panchayat, and more recently in the Sahja system." (Ibid.) Thus, while some pronouncements represent welcome indications of a movement in the direction of a redistribution of power, they do not, as yet, go very far in implementation.

The recognition of the political nature of participation raises two immediate issues - the specification of the appropriate political organisations to articulate various interests, and, given proportional representation, an electoral system by which the distribution of seats are determined for each level in the political sphere. The first will clearly be under constant review by the participants themselves, as new problems demand the re-evaluation of interests and alliances. However, as a start, the following is one categorisation of the deprived according to differing interests in the political economy of Nepal. This categorisation derives both from our analysis of conflict in the political economy as well as from recent experience, albeit limited, in the official "class" organisations in Nepal before their recent loss of constitutional status. Two of these "class organisations" were for "workers" and "Peasants". Parts of these previously undifferentiated organisations could form the basis of organisations to express the interests of:

a) landless agricultural labourers;

b) small peasants (say, up to ½ hectare)

(Previously the "Peasants" Organisation included all owners of land irrespective of size of holding). and;

c) urban labourers.

In each of these organisations, a certain number of positions could be reserved for women from these groups (possibly in place of the present separate "Women's Organisation"). These organisations would perform functions normally performed by trades unions in other countries as well as forming constituencies for political organisation but would require some central funding given the poverty of households in these groups.

The administrative means of fixing the number of seats needs adequate information from the relevant organisations about the numbers of the population in each category, which is sufficiently accurate and proof against gross falsification. The first two categories, above (constituting about 80 per cent of the total population of the country) could be identified according to land registration records and this information added to the electoral register; alternatively, their status could be self-defined and registered. Non-agricultural workers can easily be counted for each *panchayat* by returns from licensed establishments employing ten or more workers (which already exists at town *panchayat* offices). Smaller establishments could be obliged to file information on names of regular employees. In effect, there will probably occur some double-counting since even regular employees, as our own studies have indicated, maintain their rural ties and may be included in the electoral register in the countryside. But manipulation in terms of false declarations are most likely (if our filed observations on the impact of present manipulations of the electoral system are generalisable) by those whose monopoly of power is threatened. This alliance with the bureaucracy is such that the only protection for those presently excluded is opening the whole process to public scrutiny.

The restoration of rights of "combination and association" would use the different and competing interests that *exist* within the political economy of Nepal to facilitate this scrutiny. Part of the "class organisation's" role would be to select candidates for elections, scrutinise the electoral process, and exercise rights of recall on successful candidates at all levels of government up to and including the National Assembly. Direct elections to the District and National Assemblies are not part of the present *panchayat* system. Village elections have recently been restored after a brief period of nomination by District level Back to the Village Campaign officials appointed directly from the Palace. Popular participation in politics at the District level would help increase the effectiveness of the District *Panchayat* Development Committee. Law and order could continue to be the responsibility of the Chief District Officer (CDO), exercised under the scrutiny of a more representative National Assembly.

The central question for us is that of the pressure that certain groups may (or may not) exercise on the government to act on their behalf. The remedies for the present structural powerlessness of the disadvantaged do not lie in existing laws referring to the production of individual rights, although the existence of such laws is important. Laws regarding compensation for accidents at work (Nepal Industrial Workers Regulation 1977-78, 1st amendment), regarding minimum wages, working hours, health and safety in factories (Nepal Factory Workers Act, 1969-70), inheritance laws safeguarding the interests of unmarried or divorced women, etc. are on the statute books, but all our fieldwork throws doubt on their effective application without assistance from sympathetic organisations. This results in individual cases of great hardship and exceptional deprivation and in a more general situation where workers know that their inferior contractual position in any negotiation over pay, rights, compensation, etc. will not be improved by an inaccessible legal system. In the few cases where the very poor have taken cases to court alone, they, in our experience, lost and incurred great expense.

To make laws already in existence accessible to the people, enhanced political rights suggested above will allow the *panchayat* and "class organisations" to make the relevant aspects of the law known, and to provide legal aid in certain cases. But here again, beyond the need for legal aid is the right to some degree of collective action and the representation of the interests of the disadvantaged and deprived in institutions of their own choice and by a free press. The creation of new institutions to act, directly and indirectly, on behalf of the disadvantaged would be an important departure.

Training Local Cadres

Whilst we have already argued for strong representation of "the poor" in decision-making and local politics, and stressed the self-help aspects of development there is a vital complementary need for training and technical instruction, which at present the "development administration" is unable to provide. This seemingly harsh judgement is not made merely on the basis of a review of current programmes and actual (as opposed to nominal) levels of manning of the various development agencies, but from the view of the population which is supposed to benefit. The dismal statistics of State assistance of any sort to the less advantaged households have been documented above from our fieldwork. The case is not for yet more offices and career administrators, but for the utilisation of other sources of manpower who can provide training, temporary "leadership" and inspiration at the outset of local development projects and accept a primary responsibility to the people they are assisting. We identify three possible under-utilised sources.

The National Development Service, under which all university students are currently required to undertake one year's service in villages, is an excellent way of using student's motivation. Their work could be greatly assisted by "crash" courses in, say, simple medicine, public health, erosion control, forestry, chicken rearing, fruit-tree planting and care, or basic training in storage techniques, with specialisation wherever necessary. The total period of duty might therefore increase to be in the order of 18 months, and would be an integral part of the students' degree course. Foreign volunteer programmes stressing drinking water provision were observed operating successfully in West Central Nepal on this kind of basis.

Associated with this programme could be training of local leadership drawn particularly from among the lower classes. It would be helpful if members of the village and district *panchayats* were sent to the *same* training courses as students preparing to take their National Development Service. Regional training centres could then arrange to have students and members of the *panchayats* for which they would serve to attend at the same time. Again, worthwhile experience already exists, in this case from foreign aid projects using short-training courses for ex-servicemen to gain contact with a village and encourage self-help projects.

The number of aid projects in Nepal is relatively large, and as a result there are considerable numbers of Nepalese counterparts, research assistants, surveyors, etc. who receive training in some aspects of development. A common register of such personnel including details of their duties, duration of service, and existing skills could be maintained by aid agencies. These personnel would then be able to apply for 6-9 month bursaries to train in the same establishment as students and local people, and to serve as a temporary government official in village development activities. Such a term of service could also be an accredited qualification for government service on a permanent basis should he/she so wish.

The question of aid projects and aid agencies raises wider questions which are only peripheral to this report. We would hope that every agency is reviewing policy in the light of the "basic needs" orientation and rural development in Nepal. Questions arise on the form of rural development programmes that the agencies adopt, and their relationship with each other, their national governments/international parent organisations, and the Government of Nepal. Whatever institutional form aid takes the aid agencies must be prepared to insist to the limits of non-interference on changes in policies in the directions indicated previously. The massive importance of aid in Nepal makes it certain that aid agencies can have a positive influence if they are prepared to insist on policies likely to encourage the developments necessary if "basic needs" are to be fulfilled for the mass of the people of Nepal. This is especially true when opportunities to undertake comprehensive rural development policies exist for all the major agencies. Such policies contain immense possibilities of helping the deprived to help themselves both at the local and the national levels. As we have argued previously, any attempt to intervene must, if it is to have any chance of achieving its objectives, be based on an analysis of the balance of social forces at any given point in time which will allow the identification of likely sources of support for and resistance against basic needs programmes, whilst fully recognising the particular and social interests of the deprived themselves.

The Conclusions of this Report

The reappraisal of politics in Nepal in the late seventies, culminating in the forthcoming referendum on the Constitution in 1980, has produced an exceptional opportunity for those committed to a broad basic needs approach to develop a concerted programme for integrateddevelopment. Such a concerted effort will inevitably have to overcome new tensions at all levels, for instance between aid agencies and their diplomatic missions, "modern bureaucrats" and their more conservative colleagues and, in the towns and villages of Nepal, between the deprived and other social groups.

But the authors believe that reports currently being produced on "basic needs" and rural development will make some impact. Thus, our approach is to make a contribution to the analysis of the predicament of the people of Nepal, and to inform those (both Nepalese and foreign) who recognise the seriousness of this predicament and who are in a position to do something about it.

Our argument is that a "basic needs" strategy must be based on an analysis of deprivation and its causes. The latter include non-participation in selection of priorities, and the decision to fulfill them; restricted access to the means of production for many Nepalese; very little control over the way in which these means are used; the exclusion for many from the fruits of production other than sufficient to reproduce themselves under conditions of great hardship. No set of policies, collection of projects or other form of State action will succeed unless they assist the Nepalese disadvantaged in a progressive fashion to combat the crucial constraints on economic and social development which our field work has revealed.

The report's basic thesis is that without popular participation "basic needs" cannot be defined, let alone met. In this report we are concerned primarily with the experience of the disadvantaged, but we see their experience as part of a wider crisis which affects the whole population of Nepal. This crisis is rapidly deepening, and, as independent academics without links of a professional or direct economic or political nature, we have taken the opportunity to say directly what other reporters can only say or write about in a piecemeal fashion. In addition, we have attempted to identify such levels as exist to initiate these changes by encouraging the use of the existing limited organs of popular participation and agencies specifically concerned with the conditions of the deprived.

In the particular circumstances of the kind analysed in this report, we believe that whatever influence foreign aid donors can exert upon, and aid they can offer to, the government to help bring about the changes suggested is important, given the critical state of the economy and the situation of the mass of the people. If structural change does not take place now, then the need for famine-relief and other "last-ditch" measures may become general within the next decade. Action on the part of aid agencies must take account of any changes in the stance of the Nepalese Government. The growth of the "basic needs" philosophy in government circles in Nepal can be actively encouraged; and there is some reason to believe that such action will have a degree of success.

The authors were originally concerned that the substance of the critique contained in this report might remain on the unofficial, private level. But the crisis has now become so visible and so acute that official publications are appearing which are both critical of previous policies and adopting new approaches compatible with the "basic needs" approach.

Necessary changes will only be brought about slowly, by alliances of forces in which there will be a variety of interests, which will undoubtedly shift in the unfolding of Nepalese history over the next ten years. There should be no false optimism, given the nature of the political economy of the country, but neither should there be despair and pessimism regarding the possibilities of change in Nepal in the interests of the deprived.

BIBLIOGRAPHY

Asian Regional Team for Employment Promotion (ARTEP) (1974) *A Challenge to Nepal: Growth with Employment* (ILO, Bangkok)

Beenhakker, A. (1973) *A Kaleidoscopic Circumspection of Development Planning with Contextual Reference to Nepal* (Rotterdam University Press, Rotterdam)

Bhasin, K. and Malik,B. (1978) Small farmers of Nepal show the way' in *Bulletin 122*, No.3. (FAO, Rome)

Blaikie, P.M., Cameron, J., Feldman, D., Fournier, A., Seddon, J.D. (1976) *The Effects of Roads in West Central Nepal* (3 Vols.) (Overseas Development Group, University of East Anglia, Norwich)

Blaikie, P.M., Cameron, J., Fleming, R., Seddon, J.D. (1976) *West Central Nepal: A Statistical Guide* (Overseas Development Group, Norwich)

Blaikie, P.M., Cameron, J., Seddon, J.D. (1977) *The Effects of Roads in West Central Nepal: A Summary* (Overseas Development Group, Norwich)

Blaikie, P.M., Cameron, J., Seddon, J.D. with Fleming, R. (1977) *Centre, Periphery and Access in West Central Nepal: approaches to social and spatial relations of inequality* (unpublished report to Social Science Research Council)

Blaikie, P.M., Cameron, J.,Seddon, J.D. (1979) (forthcoming) *Crisis in Nepal: growth and stagnation at the periphery* (Oxford University Press, Oxford)

Central Bureau of Statistics, Kathmandu *Census Material* (1961, 1971)

Centre for Economic Development and Administration (CEDA) (1971) Report of Seminar on Population and Development, Tribhuvan University, Kathmandu' (CEDA, Kathmandu)

Dhital, B.P. and Yadav, R.P. (1976) Agricultural modernisation in Nepal' Seminar on Science and technology for the development of Nepal', 5th-9th September, 1976, p.10 (mimeo)

Eckholm, E.P. (1976) *Losing Ground: Environmental Stress and World Food Prospects* (W.W. Norton, New York) (particularly pp. 74-83)

Gaige, F. (1975) *Regionalism and National Unity in Nepal* (University of California Press, Berkeley)

International Bank for Reconstruction and Development (IBRD) (1973) *Economic Situation and Prospects of Nepal* Report No. 125-NEP.Asia Region, South Asia Dept., mimeo

International Labour Office (ILO) (1976) *Declaration of Principles and Programme of Action adopted by the Tripartite World Conference on Employment, Income Distribution and Social Progress and the International Division of Labour, Geneva, 4th-17th June, 1976* (ILO, Geneva) 24pp EFSGR

International Labour Office/Overseas Development Council (1977) *Employment Growth and Basic Needs: A One-World Problem* (Praeger, New York/London, XVI + 224pp)

Joshi, B.L. and Rose, L.E. (1966) *Democratic Innovations in Nepal: a case study of political acculturation* (University of California Press, Berkeley)

Materes, J. (1977) *Economic and Social Policy Synthesis Programme: Popular participation in Planning and Decision-making for Basic Needs Fulfilment: an Institutional Approach* (ILO (WEP2-32/WP 6) Geneva)

Ministry of Finance (1978) in Report of Nuwakot seminar on rural development' (Government Press, Kathmandu)

Ministry of Food and Agriculture (1962) *Agricultural Statistics of Nepal* (Kathmandu, July 1962, pp.162)

National Planning Commission (NPC) (1970) *The Fourth Five Year Plan 1970-75* (Kathmandu (English Edition 1972))

National Planning Commission (NPC) (1978) *The Sixth Five Year Plan* (Draft) (Kathmandu)

Pan, T.T.N. (1976) *Country Statement: Nepal* First Session Animal Production and Health Commission Meeting, 7th-11th June, Bangkok

Rieger, H.C., Bieri, F., Eggers, H., Godschact, W. and Steiger, J. (1976) *Himalayan Ecosystems Research Mission: Nepal Report* (South Asia Institute, University of Heidelberg, Heidelberg)

Seddon, J.d. (ed.) with Blaikie, P.M. and Cameron, J. (1976 forthcoming) *Peasants and Workers in Nepal: the condition of the lower classes* (Aris and Phillips, Warminster)

Shreshta, B.P. and Kohsin, M. (1970) A Study in the Working of Gaon Panchayats (a case study of six Gaon panchayats of Kaski District)' (Kathmandu, H.M.G. Panchayat Study Series, Vol.II)

Times of India (27th September, 1978)

United Nations Development Program (UNDP) (1978) Comments on a Strategy for Rural Development (Kathmandu)

United Nations Research Institute for Social Development (UNRISD) (1975) *Rural Co-operatives as Agents of Change: a research report and a debate* (Geneva)

Yadav, R.P. (1976) 'A glance at the present agricultural research, education and extension in Nepal' *APROSC Staff Paper No. 1, February 1976,* pp.14 (Agricultural Projects Services Centre, Kathmandu).

REFERENCES

APROSC (1993): Institutional Arrangements for Implementing Agricultural Plan Strategy Technical Paper, *Agriculture Perspective Plan Study,* Kathmandu, APROSC

APROSC (1995): *Nepal Agriculture Perspective Plan, Kathmandu,* APROSC

Blaikie, P.M. et al (1977): Centre, periphery and access in West Central Nepal; approaches to social and spatial inequality, *Report to the SSRC, Overseas Development Group,* University of East Anglia, Norwich

Blaikie, M.P. et al (1979): *The struggle for basic needs in Nepal,* Paris: OECD

Caplan, L., (1970): Land and Social Change in East Nepal: *A Study of Hindu-Tribal Relations.* London: Routledge and Kegan Paul

Conlin, S and Falk, A (1979): A Study of the Socio-economy of the Kosi Hill Area: *guidelines for planning an integrated rural development programme,* KHARDEP Report Volume 1, No.3; 131

Conlin, S. (undated circa 1980); Working paper on irrigation in Kosi Hills; *The Impact of the Kosi Hill Area Rural Development Programme:* KHARDEP, Dhankuta

Cromwell, E. et al (1992): *An Impact Assessment of the Seed Programme,* Koshi Hills Development Programme, Dhankuta

FAO Policy Analysis Division (1991): *Perspective Study of Agricultural Development for Nepal,* Rome, FAO

Gautam M., (1993): *Food security, nutrition and hygiene in Nepal,* report prepared for the World Bank, Kathmandu, 25p.

Ghimire, K., (1992): Forest or Farm? *The Politics of Poverty and Land Hunger in Nepal;* Delhi-OUP

Harriss, J., Hunter, J, Lewis, C.M. (eds) *The New Institutional Economics and Third World Development*

IIMI (1982): Proceedings of the National Workshop on Participatory Management in Agency-managed Irrigation Systems in Nepal, Department of Irrigation and IIMI-Nepal Field Operations, Kathmandu

Jones, S.F. (undated circa 1980): *Agricultural Marketing Study,* Phase 2, Volume 2, KHARDEP, Dhankuta

Kaplan, P. (Compiled) (1990): *Proceedings of the Informal Workshop on Sustainability of IRDP Activities in Nepal*

K.C., R.B. (1986): Land Reform: *Progress and prospects in Nepal,* Kathmandu: Winrock International Institute for Agricultural Development, 31p.

KHARDEP (1992): *Programme Management Office Terminal Report,* Koshi Hills Development Programme, Bangkok, ODA

Koirala, G. et al. (1992): *Proposed Approaches to Poverty Alleviation in Nepal:* Paper Presented at National Seminar on Poverty Alleviation and Human Development, Kathmandu, National Planning Commission, 22p.

Loughhead, S., et al (1993): *"Social development considerations in community forestry",* Nepal-UK Community Forestry Project, Kathmandu

Mellor, J. (1976) *New Economics of Growth,* Cornell University Press, Ithaca and London

Ministry of Agriculture (1991): *Policy outlines and immediate priorities of agricultural development for Nepal,* Kathmandu, Ministry of Agriculture, 45p.

Ministry of Agriculture Central Food Research Laboratory (1986): *Nutrition Content of Nepalese Foods,* Kathmandu, Central Food Research Laboratory, v.p.

Ministry of Agriculture, Department of Agricultural Development. Agricultural Marketing Development Section (1993) *Food balance sheet of Nepal 1991/92,* Kathmandu, Agricultural Marketing Development Section, 17p.

Ministry of Agriculture. Women Farmer Development Division (1993) Study on the *nutritional knowledge of women farmer:* a case study of Kavre district, Kathmandu: Women Farmer Development Division, 30p.

Ministry of Agriculture. Women Farmer Development Division (1993) *Women's role in production of main food crops of Nepal* (paddy, maize and wheat): baseline study in Jhapa, Chitwan, and Tanahun districts, Kathmandu, Women Farmer Development Division, 42p.

Ministry of Finance (1993) *Koshi Hills Development Programme Community Forestry Project* Annual Report 1992-1993, Kathmandu

Ministry of Supplies (1986): *Comprehensive master plan for improved food security in Nepal,* Kathmandu, Ministry of Supplies, 220p.

Nabarro, D. and Pant, M. (1983): *Description of the data collected in the second year of the KHARDEP Impact Studies* -2038-39 (1981-82); Coordinator's Office KHARDEP, Dhankuta

Nabarro, D. and McConnell, C., (1990) *Evaluation of the Impact of the Kosi Hill Area Rural Development Programme*, London, ODA

National Planning Commission (1991): *Approach to the Eighth Five Year Plan 1992-1997* Kathmandu, NPC

National Planning Commission (1991): *Country paper on nutrition programme in Nepal,* Kathmandu, NPC, 68 p.

National Planning Commission (1992): *The Eighth Plan (1992-1997),* Kathmandu, NPC, 727p.

National Planning Commission (1993): *An outline of poverty alleviation policies and programmes,* Kathmandu, NPC, 19p.

National Planning Commission Secretariat: *Central Bureau of Statistics (1994):* National Sample Census of Agriculture: Nepal 1991/92, Kathmandu, CBS, 23p.

Nepal Rastra Bank Agricultural Credit Division (1991): *Impact Evaluation of the Small Farmers' Development Programme of Nepal,* Kathmandu, Nepal Rastra Bank

Pradhan, U. et al ed. (1992): *Proceedings of the National Workshop on the Role of NGOs in Irrigation Development and Management in Nepal,* Kathmandu, IIMI-Nepal Field Operations and Udaya-Himalaya Network, Kathmandu

Pyakuryal, K.N. (1993): *APP Technical paper on Nepalese farming systems,* Kathmandu, APROSC, 39p.

Pyakuryal, K.N. (1994): *APP Technical Paper on Poverty in Nepal,* Kathmandu, APROSC, 33p.

Seddon, J.D. (1993): *"Democracy and Development in Nepal",* Discussion Paper No. 235, Norwich, School of Development Studies, University of East Anglia

Sharma, S. (1993): *Poverty in Nepal: definitions and determinants,* Kathmandu, APROSC 68p.

Siktel, P. et al (1989) Socio-economics Section PAC 1989, *"Farming Systems in the Northern Target Area of Pakhribas Agricultural Centre",* Pakhribas Agricultural Centre, Dhankuta

Thapa, G. and Banskota, M. (1993): *"Performance evaluation of selected farmer-managed irrigation systems in Nepal",* in Shaul Manor and

Jorge Chambouleyron *(ed)*, Performance Measurement in Farmer-Managed Irrigation Systems, Kathmandu, IIMI pp 95-105

Tiwari, B.N. (1990): Farm size and productivity in Nepalese agriculture: *a case study of Nawalparasi district, Kathrnandu,* Winrock International Institute for Agricultural Development 28p.

Upadhayaya, H.K. et al. (1990): *Differential adoption of modern rice technology and regional wage differential in Nepal;* Journal of Development studies vol 26 (3) p 450-468

World Bank (1990): *Nepal; Relieving Poverty in a Resource-Scarce Economy,* Washington, IBRD

World Bank (1991): *Nepal: Poverty and Incomes.* A World Bank Country Study. Washington, IBRD

INDEX